BAKERIES

A Guide to Puget Sound's Best Bakeries

A perfect day -- bicycling with friends to a great bakery.

BAKERIES BY BICYCLE

A Guide to Puget Sound's Best Bakeries

Fred Wert

Infinity Press

Seattle, WA

Published by Infinity Press,
P.O. Box 31204, Seattle, Washington 98103.

Manufactured in the United States of America.

Edited by Melissa Page
Maps by Fred Wert
Photographs by Fred Wert
Author photograph by Melissa Page
Cover design by Joan Schlichting

Library of Congress Cataloguing-in-Publication data
Wert, Fred, 1949-
    Bakeries by bicycle / Fred Wert.
    p. cm.
ISBN 1-883195-01-2
1. Bakers and bakeries -- Washington (State) -- Puget Sound region.
2. Cycling -- Washington (State) -- Puget Sound region -- Guide-books.

Library of Congress Catalog Number 93-77189

 Printed on 50% pre-consumer recycled paper

PREFACE

The combination of bicycles and bakeries is natural to anyone, like me, who has spent many rest stops on numerous bicycle expeditions eating at bakeries. Bakeries have always provided a source of delicious instant gratification, high calorie energy food and a warm, friendly atmosphere that welcomes lycra-clad bicyclists.

Bicycling by its very nature is a social activity. A stop for food enables the whole group an opportunity to talk together, instead of in the two-person conversations of the pace lines. The bakery becomes a social destination as well as a gastronomic destination, something that supermarkets cannot provide.

I spend a lot of time bicycling with a group of friends, informally called Squadro Porcello (Team Pig in Italian), whose motto is "Ride like Pig, Eat like Pig". Many of our rides focus on bakeries, including Brusseau's in Edmonds and the Sweet Life in Snohomish. These and other wonderful establishments let us drag our sweaty, tired bodies indoors and provide quality nourishment to help us ride back home. We are dependent upon their high quality bakery items for our full enjoyment of bicycling.

Baking is a labor-intensive business. I also believe that it is almost always a labor of love. Bakers are proud of their products; they get fulfillment from bringing happiness to others. I am constantly amazed at these people who get up when most of us are going to bed and cook all night to produce special treats. Many of them have done it for years. Such dedication bespeaks a love of their profession.

This book is for bicyclists and others to find their way down wonderful roads to wonderful bakeries. It is a call to everyone to patronize retail bakeries. Show them you appreciate their creations, their hard work, their expertise at baking. Help provide a steady stream of eager customers which will make it possible for them to survive, so you and I will always find a local bakery to satisfy the desire for quality baked goods.

Fred Wert
Seattle, 1993

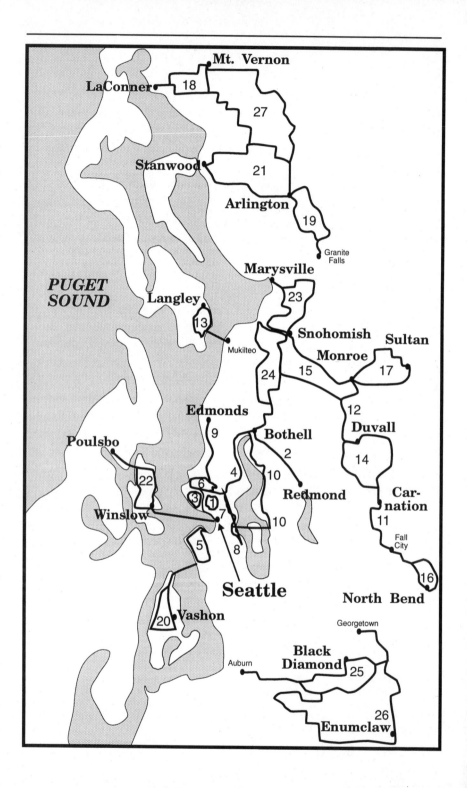

Contents

ACKNOWLEDGMENTS

I would like to thank Melissa Page for her meticulous editing of the manuscript and maps, and for helping in the research of the bakeries. Trudie Loubet, Phil Schnieder, Barbara Erwine and Lee Woods for helping with the editing. Bill Bogue and Kathy Kunz, Mark Bulgier and Laurie Foster, for helping test many of the bakeries and posing for photographs in the winter. Joe McKuen for information about bakers, baking and bakers' secrets. Nancy Poehlmann for the library cataloging information. And thanks, too, to those friends who helped in ways beyond mention . . . you know who you are.

Finally, I would like to thank all of the bakers who get up earlier than I can imagine and work long days purely for the enjoyment of others. Also, thanks to their families for whom it must be a tremendous strain.

DISCLAIMER

Bicycling on public roads involves risk. Care has been taken to select good routes, but the reader should be aware of the inherent dangers of bicycling on any road or trail.

The information on the bakeries was compiled during 1992. Some of these establishments may have closed since then or changed their hours, so please call before you go.

INTRODUCTION

THE FINEST BAKERIES

This book is, first and foremost, a guide to some of the best bakeries in the Puget Sound area. However, the fact that the selection was made by an avid bicyclist is also significant. As I have pedaled my many miles around the Puget Sound area, I have always been on the look out for good places to rest, relax and replenish my energy stores. My friends and I have patronized bakeries while bicycling because they offer high energy, fun food in relaxed atmospheres. But readers don't need to ride to the bakeries described in this book to appreciate the quality they will find there. Bicycling to bakeries will appeal to many, but eating scrumptious baked goods will appeal to almost everyone.

Puget Sound Bakeries

In the boom days of Seattle, during the 1920's, the neighborhood bakery was a common and welcome sight. There were numerous bakeries all over the region that provided the only source of bread, one of the basic foods. These bakeries developed new lines of products, many from the old country origins of their proprietors. For example, many bakeries produced the Danish and German favorites of those who settled in and around Seattle.

Some of these traditional bakeries have survived the changes in our lifestyles and shopping habits. They still produce a similar line of baked products using traditional old recipes. Bakers trained on "the Continent" still operate bakeries in our region, but the number of traditional bakeries is decreasing as bakers retire.

There is also a new type of bakery developing in the Northwest, more in line with modern lifestyles. The interest in staying physically fit, eating better and exploring new varieties of food are all part of this Northwest style. Some bakeries have opened which strive to meet the current expectations of Northwesterners. These bakeries provide whole wheat, low fat, low or no sugar products, espresso, indoor and sometimes outdoor seating, other types of light and healthy foods, and a place to socialize.

The new bakeries cater to a new group of people with different needs. They offer more than fresh bread and Danish to satisfy the diverse food interests of the Northwest eater. In some ways bakeries are providing a healthier substitute for the local bar as a place to socialize, meet people or relax in a smoke-free environment. More and more bakeries are broadening their offerings to include soups, sandwiches and a variety of drinks from the requisite espresso to micro-brewed beer.

The Best Bicycle Bakeries

The bakeries in this book were selected from the viewpoint of a bicyclist. First, they have to be reasonably accessible by bicycle, i.e., require minimal negotiation of busy roads or congested parking lots. Second, the bakeries need to have quality products worthy of the effort required to get there. All the bakeries in this book are scenically located or on a popular bicycle route. You will ride through some of the most beautiful country in the region on your way to satisfying your sweet tooth. Once you arrive, you will find a relaxed, welcoming atmosphere, even if you are a cyclist wearing lycra and cleats. And of course, every bakery in this book serves the finest quality food. Not only will you be glad you made the effort to complete the ride and try the bakery, you will want to do so again and again. There is not a bakery in this book where you can sample all the delicious treats in a single trip!

Note that by using these criteria, some of the best bakeries in the region may not have been included in this book. My apologies to those bakers who feel passed over. My goal was to provide a selection of high quality bakeries which are popular with bicyclists, not to choose bakeries solely on quality.

The selected bakeries exhibit a great variety. Some are very small with no seating, others seat 60 people with ease and carry 50 different items. Some are steeped in tradition from the old country, others demonstrate the modern Northwest lifestyle. There are many types of nationalities represented, including: Danish, Dutch, German, Chinese, Russian, French, English and American. I am always looking for more great bakeries and would appreciate any suggestions from readers. Please drop me a note, care of the Publisher's address on the order form in the back of the book.

Bakery Etiquette for Bicyclists

Please be considerate of these bakers. They work all night so that you can have wonderful fresh-baked goodies in the morning. Please don't take over all the seating, make a line at the restroom door, ask for cold bottled water for your water bottles or skate across the tiled floor on your cleats. If your group consists of more than two or three, do not all step up to the counter together -- it can make the waitstaff panic. Show the bakers and their staffs how much you enjoy their products by being considerate and they will welcome you back.

Chocolate cake from Alki Bakery.

BICYCLING

Bicycle Routes to Bakeries

For the most part, the rides were created with bakeries as the destinations. Each route was selected to provide a ride of reasonable distance, on a safe, interesting loop and with a start and finish at one of the bakeries in the book. This makes it possible for groups of bicyclists to gather and socialize before setting out on a ride, or to socialize and swap stories before breaking up for the day. The routes are also designed so that rides can be linked together in order to make longer rides.

In designing these routes, every attempt was made to avoid steep hills -- a difficult task in the Puget Sound region. While all of the rides can be ridden in the opposite direction, in some cases you may encounter significantly more difficult hills or traffic problems.

Rating the Rides

Difficulty ratings are not easy to develop. What is easy for a seasoned strong rider may be almost impossible for someone who rides only a few times per year. At the beginning of each ride is an overall classification of easy, moderate or difficult. Most of the difficult ratings are due to steep or numerous hills rather than distance. The best way for readers to determine what the rating scale means for them is to try some rides starting with the easy rides and working their way up in difficulty. Remember that steep hills can often be more difficult than long miles. As you ride more you will get stronger, especially if you eat profusely at all the bakeries you pass. I have also provided the total mileage and an elevation profile to assist readers in making their own appraisals.

The routes were selected to appeal to the broadest range of cyclists' abilities. If you are a beginner, start out with the shorter, flatter routes and work through the rides of increasing difficulty. If the rides seem too easy, string several rides together. To put together longer rides, refer to Appendix B which contains descriptions on how to connect rides.

City Rides

The city rides are designed to guide you on great bicycle rides through cities, to show you how to get to great bakeries and to provide the opportunity to get in shape for longer, more difficult rides. Most of the rides are loop rides. All of these rides start at public places with parking to facilitate the gathering of groups. Feel free to improvise. Start riding from home and bicycle to wherever on the loop suits you best. Most of the city rides pass several bakeries, so you may want to choose a different starting point depending on which bakery you want to sample. Different starting points can make riding the same loop fresher.

Country Rides

The country rides are designed to guide you between communities and from bakery to bakery. Many of the rides start at bakeries so you can fill up before starting your ride. They range from easy to difficult and cover a wide area of western Puget Sound.

Many of the rides end at the start of another ride so that you can easily create longer rides. Use the descriptions and map in Appendix B to put together longer rides.

Safe Bicycling

Bicycling is a relatively safe sport, but there are precautions that everyone should observe. First, always wear your helmet. If an accident does happen, a helmet will help minimize the damage. Second, ride responsibly and predictably. Ride with traffic, obey traffic laws and keep to the right of the lane (except where opening car doors may nail you). The more bicyclists work to cooperate with motor vechicle operators, the better treatment they will receive. Third, be prepared with adequate clothing, water, food and equipment. Fourth, make sure your bicycle is in good mechanical repair: for example, the tires are not worn out, brakes work well, derailleurs are adjusted and wheels are true. Fifth, don't draft other cyclists you don't know and never overlap the rear wheel of the bicyclist in front of you with your front wheel. If he or she suddenly moves over, you will crash. Sixth, while riding, spend most of your attention on the riding, including: the road surface, traffic, weather, grades and other bicyclists. Give bicycling the attention it requires so it will continue to be a fun and safe recreational activity.

Eating and Bicycling

Obviously, this guide puts a lot of emphasis on food. All of the rides are organized around one of my favorite bakeries and, if you limit yourself to doing rides of 10 to 15 miles, your biggest problem will be trying not to eat too many of the delicious pastries available. However, hard as it may be to believe, once you get into some of the longer, more strenuous rides, eating enough and often enough is something you need to think about.

As rides get longer, it is important to replenish your energy supply. Pedaling a bicycle for three or more hours is not the same as sitting in a car for that length of time. You are working constantly and burning calories at a steady pace. You should eat frequently, even if you are not really hungry. Many people deplete their energy supplies long before they have recognizable signs of hunger. If you don't feel hungry after 20 miles of continuous riding, eat something anyway. You will perform much better for a much longer time if you do.

On longer rides, drinking frequently is perhaps even more important than eating regularly. When bicycling, your sweat evaporates quickly and you may not realize that you have lost much water, but hard riding and hard breathing both will cause you to get dehydrated. Your efficiency as a rider decreases as you get dehydrated. Don't wait until you are noticeably thirsty. Drink often enough to polish off a water bottle approximately every 20 miles. Drink more often if it is very hot.

Equipment

Bicycling is basically a very simple sport. The two pieces of equipment that are essential are the bicycle itself and an ANSI approved bicycle helmet. Beyond that, you can get as fancy as you wish. However, as your rides get longer, a couple of items make bicycling a lot more comfortable: bicycle shorts and bicycle shoes. The former are specially designed to prevent the chafing and rubbing that long periods in the saddle can create. The latter protect your feet from the constant pressure against the pedal. While neither is necessary, both will make your longer mileage a lot more comfortable.

Repairs

Many people go for years without having to do repairs on the road. Others may have three flat tires on a single ride. Since it is impossible to know in advance what your luck will be, it is always a good idea to take a minimal tool kit along. This kit should include: tools to repair a flat (hand pump, patch kit and spare tube), allen wrenches to fit your bike parts, a small screwdriver to adjust derailleurs and a rag to wipe your dirty hands before you begin eating again. Other useful items are a chain tool and freewheel tool.

Bicycles and Ferries

Three of the rides in this book include ferry trips, scenic adventures in themselves. As a bicyclist, there are several things you should be aware of when taking the ferry. First, it does cost more to take a bicycle than to walk on. Second, you must purchase your ticket at the vehicle booth, not the passenger booth. Third, you are allowed and expected to board first and depart first. Please do not run over or scare the foot passengers who are sharing this privilege with you or we may all be banned to the rear of the boat. Fourth, when loading be extremely careful of the ramps onto the ferry and the steel deck since these can be extremely slippery if wet and often have a layer of oil on them. The danger continues if you try to walk on the steel deck or stairs with cleats. This could be the most dangerous part of the ride. Note that cleats are not allowed on the passenger decks of most ferries. Fifth, when departing, ride single file on the far right edge of the road because the cars coming behind you are all in a big hurry. An even better strategy is to pull over to the side of the ferry dock or off the road to let all the cars go by. You will then have many fewer cars passing you as you begin your ride, which will make both you and the car drivers happier.

Bicycle Organizations

Many of the wonderful advantages that make road cycling so enjoyable today are the result of hard fought battles in the government's bureaucratic jungle. Bike lanes, bicycles being allowed on ferries, the I-90 bike path, the Burke-Gilman Trail -- these are all the results of bicyclists' volunteer efforts. You can help repay your debt to those who have carried the banner in the past by getting involved. There are many options available to you. Join your local bicycle club. Participate in their government affairs committee. Go to local public hearings concerning bicycle issues. Volunteer with your local government agency to help on bicycle user counts, reviewing bicycle plans or conducting bicycle rodeos for kids. The only way we will continue to have bicycle-friendly roads and public facilities is by showing that bicycling is important to a great many people who live in the Puget Sound area.

HOW TO USE THIS BOOK

The rides in this book are organized into two groups: city rides and country rides. Within each section, rides are arranged from least to most difficult. For each ride there is a description of each bakery along the route, the hours when it is open and what you will find. Some of these bakeries may change their hours or close so we have included the telephone number. Call ahead to confirm hours and please let them know if you are bringing a big crowd. Note that some are closed Sundays or even Saturdays. The descriptions try to give you a feel for the type of place you will find, the atmosphere and the types of baked products. I have tried to mention aspects which may be important to bicyclists such as restrooms or seating.

Below the bakery descriptions are the ride descriptions. The introduction is a brief overview of the type of ride along with the starting point, distance in miles and difficulty level. The three basic difficulty ratings are easy, moderate and difficult. I have included some information explaining why these ratings apply such as hills, traffic or distance. Below this introduction is a mileage-based log of each of the turns involved in the ride. The phrase "continue right" means that the name of the street or road does not change but the

Large bakery items from the Sultan Bakery.

direction changes significantly. The phrase "angle" means it is not a ninety degree turn. I have also included "CAUTION!" notes where there are situations which require extra attention.

In addition, each ride also has a map which shows the route and the preferred direction of travel for loops. I suggest you take along additional maps if you do not know the area or it is your first trip on this route. The abbreviations used on the maps are summarized below:

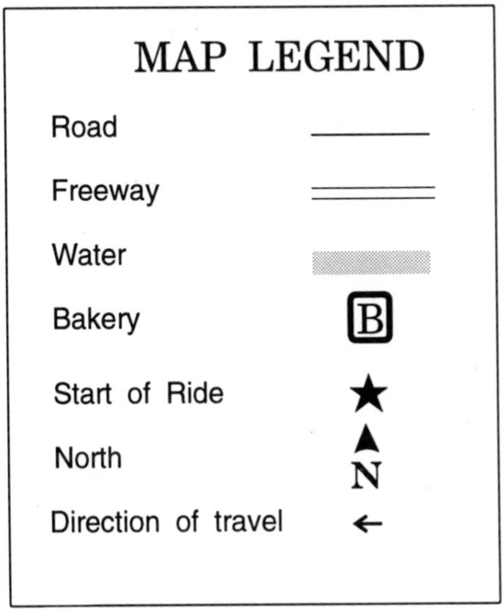

MAP LEGEND

Road	————
Freeway	════
Water	▬▬▬
Bakery	Ⓑ
Start of Ride	★
North	▲ N
Direction of travel	←

Appendices

Appendix A lists all of the bakeries included in this book. Each entry has a complete address, phone number, days and hours open, ride number and directions for driving to the location.

Appendix B contains a listing of how rides can be linked together to make longer rides. You can create your own longer routes by connecting rides described in the text.

CITY BAKERIES

A La Francaise
A Piece of Cake
Alki Bakery
Baker's Beach
Ballard Baking Company
Blake's Bakery
Boulangerie
Brusseau's
Cornerstone Desserts and Espresso
Crawford's Bakery Cafe Company
Daily Grind
Dulce's Pastry and Cafe
Exquisite Desserts
French Pastry Place, Ltd.
Frombach's Old Home Bakery
Grand Central Bakery
Great Harvest Bread Company
Greenwood Bakery Cafe
Hillcrest Bakery
Honeybear Bakery
Le Panier Very French Bakery
McGraw St. Bakery
Pert's, A Deli on Leschi
Piroshky, Piroshky
Still Life in Fremont Coffee House
Stoll's Madison Park Bakery
Store Next Door, The
Three Girls Bakery
Tio's Bakery and Cafe
Upper Crust Bakery

CITY RIDES

Melissa enjoying the view from Queen Anne.

RIDE 1

QUEEN ANNE VISTAS

To the cyclist, Queen Anne is an imposing Mt. Everest, a formidable hill climb from all sides. However, the climb is worth the effort for two reasons: first, you get a great 360 degree view of Seattle; and second, you get to taste the wonderful bakery goods produced at the McGraw St. Bakery.

McGRAW ST. BAKERY

Owner: Jessica Reisam
Address: 615 W McGraw St.,
Queen Anne Neighborhood, Seattle
Phone: 284-6327
Hours: Mon-Fri 7am-6pm; Sat-Sun 8am-6pm

The McGraw St. Bakery feels like a neighborhood bakery, a wonderful blend of old and new. The best word to describe this place is eclectic. The decor starts with a quaint brick front and instantly turns into flamboyant artwork inside, music switches from classical to Bonnie Raitt and the food ranges from cinnamon rolls to tortarustica.

The building that the McGraw St. Bakery occupies has been a bakery since the early 1920's. Jessica has retained the old brick Rainier Oven and the old neon bakery sign, but the interior has taken on a new life of its own. It is decorated with many items produced by the staff and the decorations change with staff members' moods as well as the seasons.

The specialty that makes this bakery famous is the mazurkas. While there are mazurka imitators, none approach the richness and smoothness of Jessica's Homespun Mazurka Company mazurkas. The word mazurka comes from the name of a Polish dance and from a Polish pastry. The mazurkas have become a favorite in the northwest, especially the espresso flavored variety. They are dense, sweet bars with a crumb base, smooth filling and crumbly topping. Mazurkas are the ideal bicyclist's food and were a hit one year for the annual Seattle to Portland bicycle ride.

There are more than 70 different items to choose from at the McGraw St. Bakery. Some items will not be found at many other bakeries, including:

prune danish (an east coast favorite), fresh pear danish, chocolate and cinnamon danish, fig bars, apricot bars, granola, cheese and dill brioche, cardamom sour cream coffee cake, coffee coffee cake, cheese and scallion scones, kuchen (sour cream yeast bread of German origins) and a vegetable tart called tortarustica.

You will find espresso, coffee, day-old goods, restrooms, a counter with stools and an adjacent room with tables and chairs that in good weather opens directly onto the sidewalk. This is a very popular bakery on weekends and often seating space is at a premium.

THE RIDE

This ride takes you on a tour of the fantastic views available in all directions from Queen Anne. If you start from the top, it is an easy ride with no steep hills and views, views, views. I have also shown three different approaches on the map to get up to the top of Queen Anne. These climbing routes are definitely uphill, although I have done my best to identify the gentlest grades up from three sides.

Start: McGraw St. Bakery, Queen Anne Neighborhood, Seattle. From I-5, take the NE 45th St. exit 169. Turn west and stay on NE 45th St. to Aurora Ave. N. Turn left (south) on Aurora Ave. N and cross the Aurora Bridge. Immediately across the bridge, turn right on Queen Anne Dr. and follow the arterial to Queen Anne Ave. Cross Queen Anne Ave. and angle left on W McGraw Pl. Continue right on W McGraw Street to the McGraw St. Bakery at 615 W McGraw St. on your left. Park on the street.

Miles: 4.6

Difficulty: Easy (if you drive to the bakery!).

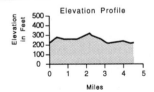

OPTIONAL APPROACHES

North: Starting at the south side of the Fremont Bridge, turn right on Florentia St. and left on 3rd Ave. W, intersecting the route at mile 3.2.

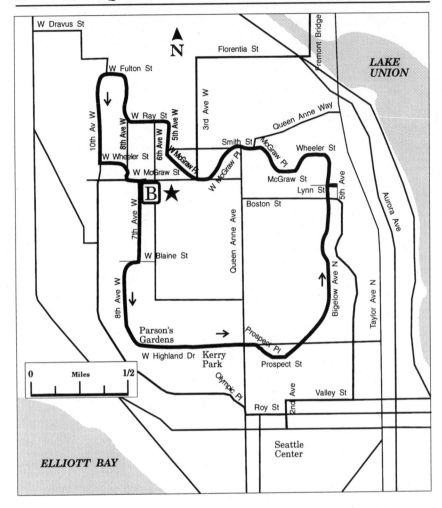

Southeast: Starting at Seattle Center, go north on 2nd Ave. N, right on Valley St., left on Taylor Ave. N and intersect the ride at mile 2.2.

Southwest: Starting at Seattle Center, go north on 2nd Ave. N, left on Roy St., right on Olympic Pl., right on 10th Ave. W and intersect the ride at mile 4.5, turning right on W McGraw St. to get to bakery.

0.0   Start at the McGraw St. Bakery. Head south on 7th Ave. W.

0.4   Right on W Blaine St., keeping to the left on the street that stays level and continue left on 8th Ave. W.

0.8   Continue left on W Highland Dr. Parsons Gardens park is on the left.

1.1   Kerry Park is on the right. Great views of downtown Seattle.

1.3   Cross Queen Anne Ave. and veer right on Prospect Pl. that continues left onto Prospect St.

1.5   Continue left on Bigelow Ave. N.

2.2   Cross Boston St.

2.25 DETOUR: Right on Lynn St. and then left on 5th Ave. Stop here and lean your bike against the guard-rail and enjoy the fantastic sweeping view of Lake Union, Capitol Hill, Wallingford, the University of Washington, Lake Washington and the Cascade Mountains. On a clear day you can even see Mt. Baker way to the north, its white peaked tip on the horizon. Then double back to Bigelow Ave. N and turn right.

2.5   Continue left on Wheeler St. Angle left on McGraw Pl.

2.6   Continue right on McGraw St. crossing bridge over Wolf Creek. The creek below is part of the City of Seattle's Natural Area Program and will never be developed.

2.7   Angle right on W McGraw Pl.

2.8   Angle left onto Smith St.

2.9   Continue straight on Smith St. CAUTION! Watch for fast cross traffic on the right that does not have a stop sign.

3.0   Cross Queen Anne Ave.

3.05 Angle left on W McGraw Pl., then continue right onto W McGraw St.

3.2   Cross 3rd Ave. W and angle right on W McGraw Pl.

3.4   Continue right on 5th Ave. W.

3.5   Continue left on W Raye St.

3.7   Continue right on 8th Ave. W.

3.9   Continue left on W Fulton St.

4.0   Continue left on 10th Ave. W.

4.4   Left on W Wheeler St.

4.45 Right on 8th St. W.

4.5   Left on W McGraw St.

4.6   McGraw St. Bakery is on your right.

RIDE 2

DO THE SAMMAMISH SLOUGH

Here is an easy ride, great at any time of year and for people of all skill levels. You will ride along a multiple-use paved path between Bothell and Redmond called the Sammamish Slough Trail. Enjoy one of the few places in an increasingly developed landscape that has wide open fields on both sides.

CORNERSTONE DESSERTS & ESPRESSO

Owner:	Sam Strok
Address:	16315 Cleveland St. NE, Redmond
Phone:	883-3871
Hours:	Mon-Fri 6:30am-7pm; Sat-Sun 7:30am-6pm

Tucked into an old brick building in the old part of Redmond is a small bakery. In this intimate little space Sam Strok produces some delicious pastries. His specialties are large sugarless muffins that make a meal in themselves and large cinnamon rolls.

The atmosphere is definitely crowded. If you take off your cleats, you may ascend the narrow stairway to the loft upstairs and find a cozy place to eat. There are great old movie photographs on the walls and even a loaner library of books.

Pastry items include several flavors of the muffins, almond sticks, apple strudel, gold bars (honey and sesame seeds), snicker doodles and peanut butter cookies. In addition, there is quick espresso service, quiche, pasta salads, regular salads, sandwiches, soft drinks and cafe ole (coffee, cinnamon, chocolate, orange). You will find a bicycle rack outside, intimate indoor seating, outdoor seating (even in the winter) and restrooms. The bakery is located near Marymoor Park, home of the Marymoor Velodrome (bicycle racing track) and just a few blocks east from the Sammamish Slough Trail.

THE RIDE

This is a wonderfully easy, flat ride. You will bicycle from Bothell to Redmond on the Sammamish Slough Trail that passes through some of the last protected green-space in the area. Take your family and friends along for a delightful ride at any time of the year. Wheelsport Bicycle Shop is located one block east and one block north of the Hillcrest Bakery at NE 183rd St. and 101st Ave. NE.

Start: Hillcrest Bakery, Bothell. From I-5 take the Lake City Way exit 171. Follow SR 522 to Bothell. At the intersection of SR 522 and Bothell Way NE stay in the center lane and go straight onto Main St. The Hillcrest

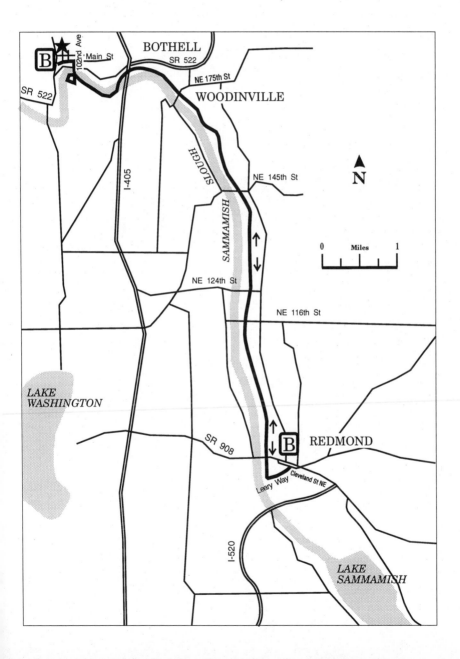

Bakery is immediately on your left. Park east on Main St. where there are no parking meters.

Miles: 18.6

Difficulty: Easy.

0.0   Hillcrest Bakery. Go left (east, uphill) on Main St.

0.1   Right on 102nd Ave NE. Cross bridge over Woodinville Dr. (SR 522).

0.2   Right into gravel parking lot for Sammamish County Park. Go across parking lot and turn right onto trail.

0.8   Cross Sammamish Slough.

0.9   Braket's Landing County Park on right next to the slough.

2.3   Pass under railroad trestle and NE 175th St. (Take trail to left if you want to get into downtown Woodinville.)

4.0   Restrooms and ballfield.

4.2   Pass under NE 145th St. (Trailhead on left. Exit here if you want to go to Chateau St. Michelle (a winery with a tasting room), which is right (west) one mile on NE 145th St.)

5.8   Pass under NE 124th St.

6.0   Restrooms, soccer fields.

6.3   Cross NE 116th St. (Trailhead on left.)

8.9   Left on Leary Way. Wood sculpture garden located on your left.

9.3   CAUTION! Cross railroad tracks carefully, turn right on Cleveland St. NE and the Cornerstone is in the building on the corner.

THE RETURN

Follow the same route in reverse.

Riders along the Sammamish Slough Trail.

RIDE 3

MAGNIFICENT MAGNOLIA

Trying to get away from home without going far from home? Take a ride around magnificent Magnolia and you will soon feel as though you've had a vacation, albeit a brief one. Here's a relatively easy ride with the city's best views up and down Puget Sound and across to the Olympics. This ride winds through beautiful Discovery Park, along the bluffs above Puget Sound and past the Chittenden Locks.

UPPER CRUST BAKERY

Owner:	Peter Larson
Address:	3204 W McGraw St., Magnolia Neighborhood, Seattle
Phone:	283-1003
Hours:	Mon-Sat 7am-5:30pm; **closed Sunday**

As befitting its name and its neighborhood, The Upper Crust Bakery is definitely a bakery of distinction. Owner Peter Larson learned the baking trade from his father and uncle who started Larson's Bakery. His pride in his work keeps him busy as the primary baker.

Specialties here trace back to Peter's Danish upbringing. His Danish pastries include: cinnamon rolls, pecan sticky buns, apple strudel and black forest cake. He is pleased to provide items requested by his customers, many of whom are quite knowledgeable about bakery products. He makes a wonderful hearty rye bread, a traditional Danish bread.

You will find several indoor tables, espresso, coffee and wonderful, fancy treats. In fine weather, take your goodies to one of the beautiful picnic spots you passed on your way to The Upper Crust and gaze while you eat.

THE RIDE

This is a relatively easy ride that earns a moderate rating because of two short, steep hills. You will travel along the eastern slopes of Magnolia near Interbay, pass by the locks, wind through Discovery Park and enjoy the fantastic views along Magnolia Blvd. W.

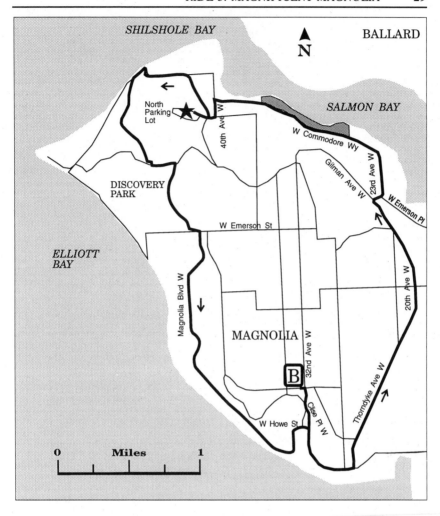

Start: North Parking lot at Discovery Park. From I-5 take the NE 45th St. exit 169 westbound to Fremont Ave. N. Turn left on Fremont Ave. N., cross the Fremont Bridge and immediately take the next right on Florentia St. Turn right on Nickerson St. and stay in the left lane. At the stop sign, turn left over 15th Ave. W and then left on W Emerson Pl. Turn right on Gilman Ave. W and follow W Government Way into the east entrance of Discovery Park. At the top of the hill take the first right down a steep downhill paved road. The parking area is to your left at the bottom of the hill.

Miles: 8.8

Difficulty: Moderate. Two short steep hills.

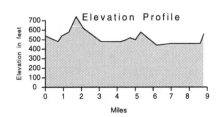

0.0   Start at the North Parking lot at Discovery Park and head east along the flat road. Take the first left with a sign that says Daybreak Star Indian Cultural Center. The intimidating signs are meant to keep cars out.

0.8   Right to viewpoint. Great views of Shilshole Marina, Whidbey Island to the north, Bainbridge Island to the west.

0.9   Right up narrow sidewalk alongside fence and up a short steep road.

1.4   Straight past intersection of two paved trails. Cross road at crosswalk and get on bicycle path.

1.5   Right at bike route sign up concrete road.

1.7   Right at next flat road (unmarked) to your right going past a number of old buildings.

2.1   South entrance to Discovery Park. Left on W Emerson St. and immediately right at the stop sign onto Magnolia Blvd. W.

3.1   Park to the right with great views to the southwest.

4.2   Continue right on W Howe St.

4.3   Left on Clise Pl. W and keep to the right at the "Y" on 32nd Ave. W.

4.5   Upper Crust Bakery is across the street to your left.

THE RETURN

4.5   Leave the Upper Crust Bakery and head back down 32nd Ave. W. Go left on Clise Pl. W.

5.0   Pass Magnolia Park on right.

5.3   Left on Thorndyke Ave. W, following Bike Route sign. Watch carefully for oncoming traffic.

6.3   Continue straight on 20th Ave. W which becomes Gilman Ave. W.

7.0   Right at stop light onto W Emerson Pl. Immediately get in left part of lane and turn left.

7.1   Left onto 23rd Ave. W.

7.5   Left on W Commodore Way.

8.2   Chittenden Locks on right. You can walk your bicycle across the locks to get to Ballard.

8.3   Commodore Park. Great views of the locks, boats and sea lions.

8.7   Left on 40th Ave. W and climb a short, steep hill.

8.8   Right into entrance of North Parking lot at Discovery Park.

RIDE 4

BURKE-GILMAN BREEZE

The Burke-Gilman Trail is one of the most popular places to ride a bicycle in the entire Puget Sound area. Not only is it free of motor vehicles, the trail is built on an abandoned railroad grade and provides a unique flat route north through the undulating landscape of NE Seattle from Ballard to Bothell. It is a great route for riders of all skill levels. The four bakeries below are not immediately adjacent to the trail, but they are close enough that they are worth the detours for great taste treats.

STILL LIFE IN FREMONT COFFEEHOUSE

Owners:	Nancy Weintraub and Ruth Quinet
Address:	709 N 35th St., Fremont District, Seattle
Phone:	547-9850
Hours:	Mon-Thurs 7:30am-9pm; Fri-Sat 8am-5pm;
	Sun 8am-12noon

A bit of the sixties still lives in what used to be funky Fremont. Designed to reproduce the coffeehouses of that era, the Still Life has a warm, cozy feeling with a mixed collection of old furniture, cafeteria-style self-service, an ever-changing art exhibit on the walls and wholesome bakery products.

The Still Life was started in 1985 to provide really delicious food of all ethnic varieties. Kim Davis does all the baking and keeps busy trying to keep the display cases full of healthy products. The recipes have come from everyone and everywhere.

The selection of baked products is primarily bars and non-traditional cakes. Hazelnut shortbread, spicy gingerbread cake, apple apricot crumble, Still Life coffee cake, toffee, lemon walnut bars, zucchini-apricot-carrot bread, banana bread, cranberry streusel with pecans, lemon poppyseed cake, pecan squares, pepper biscotti, espresso bars, chocolate zucchini cake, chocolate chip cookies, oatmeal fruit bars with prunes and golden raisins, raspberry hazelnut mazurka, fluffy coconut cake, mud cake with chocolate and espresso and German chocolate brownies are among the numerous offerings.

For those who want a change from or an addition to the sweet stuff, the Still Life serves ethnic soups, a granola, fruit and yogurt plate, sandwiches and dinner entrees. You will find Torrefazione coffee and espresso, several local micro-brew beers, wine, Cold Mountain juices, Kemper cream soda and root beer, and other soft drinks. You will also find jazz on Thursday evenings, restrooms, outside seating and a large bicycle rack out front.

A LA FRANCAISE

Owner: Joan Johnson
Address: 2609 NE University Village Shopping Center, Seattle
Phone: 524-9300
Hours: Mon-Fri 7:30am-8pm; Sat-Sun 7:30am-6pm

A La Francaise is modeled after the small, intimate French country boulangerie. Here you will find authentic French bakery goods such as croissants, baguettes and brioche. The excellent food and wonderful outdoor patio compensate for the car-oriented location.

The bakery was started in 1982 by a group interested in creating a quality French-style bakery. Joan Johnson and her husband, the current owners, have worked hard to continue to provide fresh and flavorful products that delight the taste buds. Their bakers use the highest quality ingredients they can obtain. They are particularly proud of their croissants, offered with a variety of fillings. The pain au dulce (bread with raisins) is an example of a nutritious non-fat goody. Other items include: fruit tarts, apricot pinch, spinach and tomato rolls, pizza, rolls, muffins and cookies.

You will find espresso, Starbucks coffee, classical music, limited inside seating on stools and a nice outdoor courtyard.

GREAT HARVEST BREAD COMPANY

Owners: Maggie and Jeff Weisman
Address: 171 Bothell Way NE, Lake Forest Park
Phone: 365-4778
Hours: Mon-Fri 7am-9pm; Sat-Sun 7am-6pm

A new bakery based on high quality whole wheat goodness, the Great Harvest Bread Company in Lake Forest Park is a great place for a bicyclist to visit. Here you will find whole wheat bakery products which are healthy, tasty and attractive.

While the location is new, the Weisman's have been in the baking business since 1985 when they opened their original store in Laurelhurst. They are very proud of the quality of their products and it shows. Their wheat comes from Three Forks Montana and is ground in the bakery to insure freshness. Grinding their own whole wheat flour also reduces the need for oils as the flour is still moist from the grinding. All breads are formed by hand and if you arrive before noon you can watch the bakers at work.

As befits its name, the Great Harvest Bread Company specializes in bread. Breads available every day are molasses whole wheat, raisin whole wheat, sprouted whole wheat, honey whole wheat, sunflower whole wheat, oat bran wheat and Country French. Their specialty breads are apple walnut, cherry walnut, dill onion rye, golden wheat, potato herb, jalapeno corn bread, pumpernickel, spicy date nut, tomato herb, sour dough and light wheat egg dough. You will also find foccacia (a huge French loaf smothered in olive oil, sundried tomatoes, cheeses, herbs and garlic), challah, hamburger and hot-dog buns, cheesesticks, soft bread sticks and croutons.

The Great Harvest Bread Company may specialize in breads, but the hungry bicyclist will find many other items to choose from. Two non-bread specialties are cinnamon rolls (with raisins and nuts or plain) and whole wheat scones. Also try the croissants with various fillings such as raspberry peach, danish, energy bars (chocolate, nuts, raisins), Bob's power bars (peanut butter, raisins, sunflower seeds, oats, sugar), brownies (three kinds of chocolate with a little flour), muffins, large cookies (they also come in six-packs), macaroons and gingerbread people.

You will find coffee, espresso, stand-up counters inside, inside wooden benches and small tables, outside sheltered seating, a bike rack and plenty of whole wheat bakery products.

HILLCREST BAKERY

Owners: Lyda, Peter and Bob Kaskes
Address: 10010 Main St., Bothell
Phone: 486-5292
Hours: Mon-Fri 6am-6pm; Sat 6am-5pm; **closed Sunday**

The Hillcrest is a family-run, community bakery that has survived amidst the dramatic growth in and around Bothell. The Kaskes serve a huge selection of traditional Danish bakery products.

Lyda Kaskes and her sons Peter and Bob do all the baking for this very busy bakery. The number of products is mouth watering. They have fancy cakes, breads, doughnuts, cookies, muffins, scones, apple streusel, pies, danish, coffee cakes and fruit bars. You have to see it to believe it!

Gingerbread house built by Hillcrest Bakery.

Not satisfied with the wide array of goodies they produce all year long, the Kaskes make a special treat for the community each Christmas season. Bob and Peter build a huge, walk-in gingerbread house made of more than 700 pounds of real gingerbread. Even if the weather is too cold and damp for bicycle riding in December, make sure you get to Bothell to see this amazing sight. Kids of all ages will love it.

At the Hillcrest Bakery, you will find booths inside, a bench outside and friendly service.

THE RIDE

The ride along the Burke-Gilman Trail is one of the most popular rides in Seattle. This route takes you from the current western terminus in Fremont

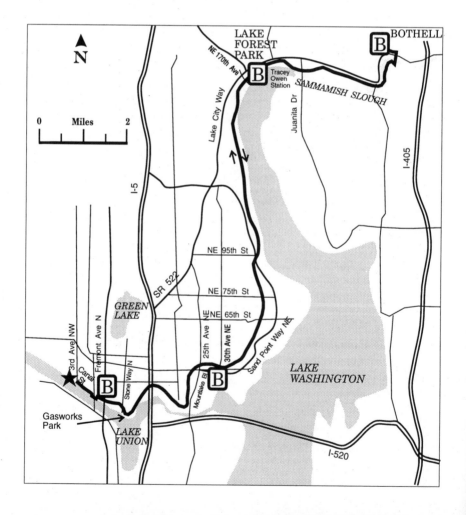

to Bothell, the official eastern end of the trail. You will need to leave the Burke-Gilman Trail to get to the bakeries, but each detour is worth the effort.

Start: Begin at 3rd Ave. NW and the Lake Union Ship Canal, the western end of the Burke-Gilman Trail. From I-5, take the NE 45th St. exit 169, turn west and follow to Fremont Ave. N. Turn left on Fremont Ave. N and at the bottom of the hill, turn right one block before the main light in Fremont on N 36th St. Continue straight on N 36th St. and turn left on 1st Ave. NW. The Burke-Gilman trail is straight ahead. The 3rd Ave. NW starting point is to your right. Park along N Canal St. next to the trail.

Miles: 39.6

Difficulty: Easy. Flat and you can turn around at any distance.

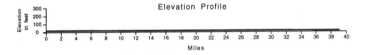

0.0   Start along the north side of the ship canal on N Canal St. and head east. The Burke-Gilman Trail officially starts at 3rd Ave. NW.

0.3   Exit the Burke-Gilman Trail paved portion onto N Canal St.

To go to the Still Life Cafe in Fremont Coffeehouse

Continue east on N Canal St. past the sign saying DO NOT ENTER (for cars) up to Fremont Ave. N. Cross Fremont Ave. N and N 34th St. Using the crosswalks is the safest way. Left on Fremont Ave. N then right on N 35th St. The Still Life in Fremont Coffeehouse is on your right. To continue, return to the intersection of Fremont Ave. N and N 34th St. Cross N 34th St. to the island where the wonderful statue called "Waiting for the Interurban" is located. Head east on the bike lane on N 34th St. to Stone Way N.

If not going to the Still Life

0.4   Immediately turn right off N Canal St. into a small parking lot and head east through a cyclone fence gate. Just past the large blue building on your right, turn right and then left. Continue straight through the hole under the Fremont Bridge approach and follow the painted stripes on the pavement. Just past the support towers for the Aurora Bridge, turn left enter the Burke-Gilman Trail which takes you to Stone Way N.

1.0   Cross Stone Way N. Continue on the Burke-Gilman trail.

1.5   Gasworks Park is on your right. This is an alternate starting point and there are public restrooms.

2.8   Cross 15th Ave. NE in the University District.

3.4   Pass Hec Edmundson Pavilion on your right. There is a bridge over Montlake Blvd. if you want to head south across the Montlake Bridge.

4.4   Cross 25th Ave. NE.

To go to A La Francaise

At mile 4.6, turn right on 30th Ave. NE and turn right at the sign "University Village Entrance." Just after the stop sign at the bottom of the hill, turn left into the parking area behind the shops. Continue straight until the end of the parking lot and then turn right and go straight into the courtyard. Please walk your bicycle or ride around the buildings on your left to get to the other end of the courtyard. A La Francaise is located at the far end of the courtyard on the left (south) side. Return the same way you came to continue on the Burke-Gilman Trail.

If not going to A La Francaise

4.6   Cross 30th Ave. NE.

7.7   Pass under a bridge with stairs on the right up to Sand Point Way.

10.3   Matthews Beach Park is on your right. Restrooms, access to Lake Washington.

To go to the Great Harvest Bread Company

At mile 14.3, turn left (north) on NE 170th Ave. and enter the Lake Forest Park Towne Centre. Turn right, then left. Great Harvest will be straight back. Return the way you came and continue on the Burke-Gilman Trail.

If not going to the Great Harvest Bread Company

14.3   Cross NE 170th Ave.

15.1   Tracey Owen Station park is on your right. Restrooms, access to Lake Washington, ducks.

15.9   Pass under Juanita Drive in a new tunnel, the "missing link" of the Burke-Gilman Trail.

17.9   Left onto the Sammamish Slough Trail. Take the next hard right onto the bridge over the Sammamish Slough.

18.6   Just after passing an arched wooden bridge to Bothell Landing, go straight across a gravel parking area and turn left on 102nd Ave. NE.

18.7   Left on Main St.

19.8   Hillcrest Bakery is at 10010 Main St.

THE RETURN

Follow the same route in reverse for another 19.8 miles.

Squadro Porcello on the Burke-Gilman Trail.

RIDE 5

WEST SEATTLE TOUR

This route combines four bakeries and great views for a moderately easy ride. Two bakeries, Frombach's and Blake's, represent traditional-style bakeries long popular in West Seattle. Dulce's and the Alki Bakery represent the new avant-garde style both in products and ambiance.

DULCE'S BAKERY AND CAFE

Owners: Carlos Kainz and Julie Juerrero
Address: 4100 Beach Dr. SW, Alki Neighborhood, Seattle
Phone: 933-8400
Hours: Tues-Wed 7am-6pm; Thurs-Sat 7am-9pm;
Sun 7am-3pm; **closed Monday**

Located on Puget Sound in a quiet corner of West Seattle, Dulce's Bakery and Cafe is an upscale, intimate cafe with elegant bakery items. Here you will find desserts, cakes and breakfast baked items of the highest quality. You can watch the chef work through large glass doors both from inside the cafe or from the sidewalk outside.

Carlos and Julie gained experience at one of the fancy downtown clubs and this experience shows in the quality and perfection of presentation of their baked goods, which are beautiful as well as delicious. Carlos and Julie are both of Mexican descent and offer a few Mexican items such as chilaquiles, an enchilada-style tortilla with spicy tomato sauce, chicken breast, cheese and two fried eggs on top.

Baked items include: scones, fruit compote, tartlettes, pithivier, chocolate eclairs, bread puddings from various types of bread, cheesecakes, croissants, muffins and fancy, rich cakes. The energy bars are made from molasses, coconut and oatmeal and are not too sweet. The vegetarian rollups are almost a meal in themselves.

You will find inside seating, Caffe Mauro espresso, bathrooms, fresh juices, soups and sandwiches, beer and wine, breakfast, light entrees and full dinners. In good weather, enjoy sitting outside on the wide sidewalk and gazing out across Puget Sound to the Olympics. Across the street is the Weather View Park, with public access to Puget Sound and a view west.

FROMBACH'S OLD HOME BAKERY

Owner: Joe McKuen
Address: 2332 California Ave. SW,
West Seattle Neighborhood, Seattle
Phone: 932-5574
Hours: Mon-Fri 6am-6pm; Sat 6:30am-5pm; Sun 7am-1pm

Here is a traditional neighborhood bakery just as it has been for the last 30 years in West Seattle. You will find cases full of baked products, a rotating cake display, small tables and large sidewalk windows.

Joe McKuen grew up in Philadelphia and learned to bake at a young age. His grandfather was a baker in Hungary and seven of his uncles are also bakers. He does almost all the baking himself and can produce just about any baked good you can imagine. Joe describes his baking style as "east coast," meaning he concentrates on German and Jewish products. Most of the recipes he uses were passed down from his family, although some he has created on his own. Traditional recipes include: stolen, fruitcake and strudel made with pulled dough, not puffed dough.

You will find a wide variety of traditional baked products prepared with knowledge and skill, inside seating, coffee and soft drinks. This is a bakery worth visiting on a regular basis as Joe changes the items with the seasons and as he gets new requests from his customers.

BLAKE'S BAKERY

Owner: Hanna Yuse
Address: 4737 California Ave. SW,
West Seattle Neighborhood, Seattle
Phone: 937-4554
Hours: Tues-Sat 6:30am-6pm; **closed Sunday and Monday**

The sign over this bakery says "Blake's Bakery 1856", an indication of its long history. The family baking tradition began in England and was carried to the United States in 1956 when Fred Blake opened the bakery in this West Seattle location. Eventually, the spoon passed to his son Carl Blake who recently retired in 1992. The responsibility for carrying on the Blake's tradition now belongs to Hanna Yuse, a graduate of the Culinary Institute of America (fondly known as the CIA), in Hyde Park, New York.

Joe McKuen, of Frombach's Bakery, showing his love of baking.

This is a large bakery with huge display cases and a wide variety of products. Hanna's specialties are individual pastries, sometimes called French pastries. With her German background she is making some German style breads, which are dense and heavy using sour as the leavening.

The bakery is very famous for its maple bars, chocolate mousse cakes and blueberry-cream cheese muffins. There are a wide variety of items to choose from including breads, cookies, French pastry and muffins. You will find espresso, coffee and ample seating inside.

ALKI BAKERY

Owner: Kevin Piper
Address: 2738 Alki Ave. SW, Alki Neighborhood, Seattle
Phone: 935-0616
Hours: Sun-Thurs 8am-9:30pm; Fri-Sat 8am-10pm

Alki is the Monterey of Puget Sound with sandy beaches, a wide pedestrian/bicycle/wheeled-object path, and many places to hang out. The Alki Bakery is one of the hip places to people-watch and has a northwest style. It is bright, polished and alive with a good selection of desserts and breakfast bakery goods.

The bakery was begun in 1985 as part of the Alki Restaurant. Since then, the bakery products have become so popular that they now merit their own building. There is ample table seating inside or you can sit at the window counter and look out across Alki Ave. to Puget Sound. Of course, if it's summer and you are really in a hurry, you can just pull up at its unique sidewalk service window. You don't even have to dismount from your bicycle! This window on the west side was installed to service the many non-motor vehicle customers who show up via all types of locomotion. It may also help keep the scuba divers from tracking seaweed inside.

The bakery products feature fancy cakes and some lighter items such as muffins and scones. If you are looking for a sugar rush try the triple treat chocolate cookie or the white chocolate macadamia chip cookie. For something less sweet try one of their breads such as the Rustica Italian. You will find espresso, coffee, soft drinks, restrooms, plenty of inside seating, a great view and an upscale atmosphere.

THE RIDE

This short ride has a steep hill, great views and four great bakeries. It is

The cake display at Alki Bakery.

worth doing many times at different times of the year, to enjoy the changing seasons as well as the changing baked goods. To make a longer ride, at mile 4.4 turn left and follow Beach Dr. to Lincoln Park and back. Just south of Lincoln Park is another great bakery, The Original Bakery (see Ride 20).

Start: Don Armeni Park, West Seattle. From I-5 take the Spokane Street exit and turn west on Harbor Ave. Go north and look for a large park and parking area on your right with a boat launch.

Miles: 8.4

Difficulty: Moderate. One long, steep hill.

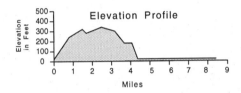

0.0	Start at Don Armeni Park on Harbor Ave. and head south. (Park on the street as the parking lot is restricted to cars with trailers between 4-8 AM and 3-5 PM. There are restrooms near the boat launch.)
0.2	Right on California Ave. SW. Climb this long, moderately steep road.
0.8	Left into Hamilton Viewpoint. This park has a great view of Seattle and gives your legs a chance to rest. Then continue on California Ave. SW.
1.5	Frombach's Old Home Bakery is on your left at 2332 California Ave. SW. Alki Bicycle Company is one block south on the west side of California Ave. SW.
1.6	Right on SW Admiral Way and proceed two blocks.
1.7	Left on 45th Ave. SW.
2.7	Left on SW Andover St.
2.75	Right on 44th Ave. SW.
3.2	Left on SW Alaska St. and then the first right onto California Ave. SW.
3.3	Blake's Bakery is on your right at 4737 California Ave. SW.
3.4	Right on SW Edmunds St. and down a steep hill.
3.7	Left on 49th Ave. SW.
3.9	Right on SW Hudson St.
4.1	Continue right on SW Jacobson Rd.
4.4	Right on Beach Dr. SW. (To get to the Fauntleroy ferry terminal turn left on Beach Dr. SW and follow it into Lincoln Park. The ferry terminal is immediately south of Lincoln Park.)

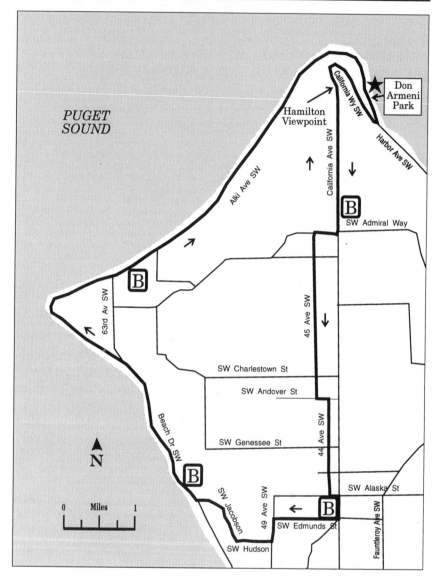

4.7   Mee-Kwa-Mooks Park is on your right. Viewpoint on beach with
       seating is on your left.
5.0   Dulce's Bakery and Cafe is on your right at 4100 Beach Dr. SW.
5.4   Continue straight on Beach Dr. SW.
5.8   Right on Alki Ave. SW.
6.3   Continue on Alki Ave. SW to the Alki Bakery which is on your right at
       2738 Alki Ave. SW.
8.4   Don Armeni Park.

RIDE 6

NORTHWEST SEATTLE SAMPLER

The north part of Seattle is a popular place for bakeries, boasting a number of new ones as well as several older ones. This ride takes you to some of the best bakeries on a moderately easy route from Green Lake, across Ballard and back through Fremont and Wallingford.

HONEYBEAR BAKERY

Owners: Carl Gaskill and Rissa Warner
Address: 2106 N 55th St., Green Lake Neighborhood, Seattle
Phone: 545-7296
Hours: Mon-Sun 6am-11pm

In just six years, the Honeybear Bakery has become a Seattle institution. Carl and Rissa moved here from the mountains of Stehekin and brought their love for baking and wholesome recipes with them. The high quality products, friendly atmosphere and great variety have made this bakery extremely popular. Don't be surprised to ride up and find the line extending outside onto the sidewalk next to the mascot, a wood-carved bear with a baker's cap.

One of the most popular items is their sourdough cinnamon roll which is large, chewy and comes with extra icing for those who just can't get enough sweets. Other favorites are pumpkin and morning glory muffins, white chocolate brownies and a good selection of large cakes of various flavors offered by the slice. They have a wide selection of whole wheat breads as well as soups, quiche, salads and rolls.

The secret to Carl and Rissa's success comes from the careful attention they give to their products. They bake in small batches and still use the unprofessional method of measuring by quantity, not weight. They use organic ingredients if available. Most of their supplies come from Bear Foods in Chelan (naturally). By baking in small batches, they are always able to have fresh hot cinnamon rolls and pumpkin muffins, their most popular products.

At the Honey Bear, the customers' requests are also taken seriously. Initially there was almost no indoor seating, but customers asked for more. Now there are numerous types of tables in two rooms, often being shared and often packed. It is a comfortable place to sit for a while and enjoy good food.

The hours have been extended every day from 6am to 11pm. In addition, live music is provided Fridays and Saturdays, recycling of materials is encouraged and soups and salads have been added -- all at the request of customers.

You will find espresso, coffee, tea, juices and sodas, salads, soups, breads and healthy baked goods. There are many tables, but they are often full, especially on weekend mornings. There are restrooms and some limited seating and a bike rack outside.

GREENWOOD BAKERY

Owners:	Mark and Marja Handman
Address:	7227 Greenwood Ave. N,
	Greenwood Neighborhood, Seattle
Phone:	783-7181
Hours:	Tues-Sat 6:30am-9pm; Sun 7am-1pm;
	closed Monday

The Greenwood Bakery is one of the real old-time neighborhood bakeries. It has existed in this location for 66 years. Mark and Marja Handman, the current owners, are committed to continuing the fine baking tradition. They have been baking for 16 years, including three years working in Holland. In addition, they are making changes guaranteed to appeal to the new Northwest style.

Mark and Marja provide a very large variety of all types of baked goods, from fancy cakes to cookies, from breads to apple beignets. They are very proud of their breads, scones and Danish pastries. There is such a variety that you are sure to find something to your liking.

A specialty here is Pithvivier, a pie-shaped pastry made of puffed pastry with an almond creme filling. It is named after a region in France and is identified by the swirling cuts in the top.

The quality and care the owners take is reflected in their exclusive use of organic flour and even imported apricot glaze from France. They are also very proud of their new French-style bread oven that produces loaves with the traditional thick, hard crusts.

The bakery is small and intimate with five tables inside and two outside on the wide sidewalk along Greenwood Ave. N. In addition to bakery products they serve espresso, coffee, pizza, quiche and soups.

BALLARD BAKING COMPANY

Owners: Mark and Marja Handman
Address: 5909 24th Ave. NW, Ballard Neighborhood, Seattle
Phone: 781-0091
Hours: Tues-Sat 7am-7pm; Sun 7am-5pm; **closed Monday**

The Ballard Baking Company is a newly remodeled old bakery. Here you will find the same fine quality products that you just sampled at the Greenwood Bakery as they share the same ownership.

The Ballard Baking Company is bright and cheery, with large windows, bright lights, art work on the walls and new pastry cases. Pastry items include: apple, marionberry, blueberry cream cheese or fresh fruit danish, four types of croissant, chocolate or cinnamon-apple beignets, bearclaws, cheese pockets, cinnamon rolls and frosted fudge brownies. Specialties include: nut rolls (croissant dough in a spiral with nuts and an apricot glaze), almond pear tartlette, chocolate hazelnut bars, creme brule (burnt cream) and cherry custard coffee cake.

In addition to the pastries, they have vegie-pockets (croissant dough filled with mixed spiced vegatables), their own bagels, quiche, a soup of the day and several sandwich choices. They produce many great breads from a new French-style oven.

You will find plenty of seating both indoors and out, restrooms, Caffe Appassionato espresso and Ballard Baking Company t-shirts. If you are looking for a picnic site, continue south and east to the Ballard Locks where there is a grassy area overlooking the lock area.

THE STORE NEXT DOOR

Owner: Julia Miller
Address: 4405 Wallingford Ave. N,
Wallingford Neighborhood, Seattle
Phone: 547-3203
Hours: Mon-Fri 7am-6pm; Sat 8am-5pm; Sun 8am-12noon

Julia Miller developed a reputation for quality, healthy food with her first restaurant, Julia's 14 Carrot Cafe. The Store Next Door follows that tradition with an attention to variety and quality.

This small store has a plethora of healthy, scrumptious offerings. There are all types of cookies, bars, muffins, cakes and tarts. Looking for calories? Try trail-mix cookies (oats, raisins, peanuts, chips), hiker bars (chocolate chips, apricots, coconut, oatmeal, dates), chewy love bars (caramel, oats, walnuts, chocolate chips), chocolate cherry brownies or raspberry linzer bars. There are always a number of interesting cakes such as black and white cheesecake, pumpkin chocolate bundt cake and lemon poppy cake.

Lower calorie selections include: chocolate orange or peach date muffins, orange pistachio or hazelnut biscotti, persimmon cookies, whole wheat scones, whole wheat cinnamon rolls and oat yogurt coffee cake. Julia also carries bagels from the Bagel Oasis, several breads and a few wheatless and/or sugarless cookies. You will find espresso, coffee, counter seating, day olds and outside sidewalk seating in nice weather.

BOULANGERIE

Manager: Marian Dam
Address: 2200 N 45th St., Wallingford Neighborhood, Seattle
Phone: 634-2211
Hours: Mon-Sun 7am-7pm

Back in 1979, Leah Grossman could not find a bakery that produced the French breads and pastries that she grew up with in France, so she returned to France, learned the baking trade and brought back a French master baker and the equipment to produce quality French baked goods in Seattle. Although she has left the Boulangerie, the bakery continues the tradition she began. The head baker, Xon Luong, learned French baking in Vietnam where bakers are highly respected in the community.

All products are made by hand and cooked in a Bongard French oven, which has a stone surface, even heat and steam sprayers to bring the characteristic thick, glistening crust to the breads. The bakers are well trained in the traditional French baker methods and their products show that training.

Pastry items include: croissants (plain and chocolate), torsade (croissant dough in a strip with jam), chausson aux pommes (apple filled croissant dough) and escagot (spiral dough with raisins and light glaze). Their breads are wonderful to see as well as taste and include: Parisien, pain aux oignons (onion), pain complet (whole wheat), seigle (rye), pain sur levain (sourdough), Joko (French white), three seed baguette, rye with raisin and rye with walnut.

Fresh loaves from the Boulangerie.

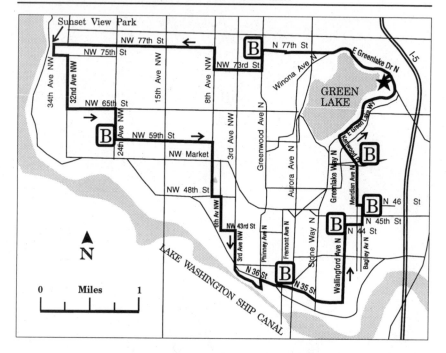

Specialties include: brie en brioche (a small round loaf with a large piece of brie cheese cooked inside), pithivier (a puffed pastry made with ground almonds and brown sugar) and pain de campagne ("bread of the country," a large hard loaf that uses a fermented starter). For a major energy boost, try the honey almond or honey walnut tarts.

You will also find espresso, a wide selection of imported and local cheeses and local papers. You will find a few chairs inside and a bench on the west side of the building. To get away from the bustle of N 45th St., take your goodies and ride north on Bagley Ave. N to the Meridian Playfield. The Bikesmith bicycle shop is located one block east on N 45th St.

THE RIDE

This ride wanders through several north Seattle neighborhoods. Starting at Green Lake you pass through Greenwood to an overlook of Shilshole, through lower Ballard to Fremont and climb back up through Wallingford. Along the way you will pass several tempting bakeries and explore some seldom-used back routes.

Start: Green Lake Community Center, Green Lake Neighborhood, Seattle. From I-5, take the NE 45th St. exit 169. Go west along NE 45th St.

and turn right on Stone Way N which becomes Green Lake Way N. Follow Green Lake Way N along the east shore of Green Lake and through the five way stop intersection, where it becomes E Green Lake Dr. N. Take the next left at the entrance to the Green Lake Community Center. Park in the parking lot. If the lot is full, there is usually additional parking available along E Green Lake Way N or E Green Lake Dr. N.

Miles: 12.3

Difficulty: Moderate. Some hills, some traffic.

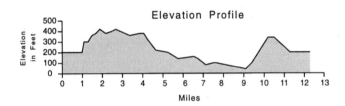

Elevation Profile

0.0   Start at Green Lake parking lot at Green Lake Community Center. Turn left on E Green Lake Dr. N.

0.5   Continue in left lane straight on E Green Lake Dr. N which becomes Winona Ave. N.

0.8   Right on N. 77th St.

1.0   Cross Aurora Ave. N, climb short hill.

1.1   Cross Linden Ave. N at top of hill.

1.3   Cross Dayton Ave. N, start up steep hill.

1.5   Left on Greenwood Ave. N.

1.7   Greenwood Bakery is on your right under a blue awning next to Ken's Market.

1.7   To continue, turn right (west) on N 73rd St (which quickly becomes NW 73rd St.).

1.9   Cross 3rd Ave. NW.

2.2   Right on 8th Ave. NW.

2.5   Left on NW 77th St.

2.9   Cross 15th Ave. NW.

3.4   Cross 24th Ave. NW. (You can push the crosswalk button to stop traffic.)

3.9   Cross 32nd Ave. NW.

4.1   Left on 34th Ave. NW. Sunset View Park, with a great view of Shilshole Marina, Alki and the Olympic Mountains, is on your right.

4.2   Left on NW 75th St.

4.3   Right on 32nd Ave. NW. CAUTION! It is difficult to see oncoming traffic from your left due to a building in the way. Stay next to the curb.

4.7   Left on NW 65th St.

5.2   Right on 24th Ave. NW.

5.4   Ballard Baking Company Cafe.

5.4   Leave Ballard Baking Company Cafe and head east on NW 59th St.

5.8   Cross 20th Ave. NW.

6.0   Cross 15th Ave. NW carefully.

6.5   Right on 8th Ave. NW.

6.7   Cross NW Market St.

7.1   Left on NW 48th St.

7.2   Right on 6th Ave. NW.

7.5   Left on NW 43rd St.

7.6   Right on 3rd Ave. NW.

7.9   Left on Leary Way NW and immediately turn right on 3rd Ave. NW, a large asphalt area, and head left and find the entrance to the Burke-Gilman Trail at the east end of the concrete plant.

8.0   Enter Burke-Gilman Trail.

8.4   Exit Burke-Gilman Trail and go left on Phinney Ave. N.

8.5   Right on N 36th St. and get in left lane **before** the corner. Then get in left turn lane for N 35th St.

8.7   Still Life in Fremont Coffeehouse is on your right (south) next to large mural on building (see Ride 4 for a description).

8.8   Continue uphill on N 35th St. heading east.

9.1   Cross Stone Way N.

9.4   Left on Wallingford Ave. N.

10.2   Store Next Door is on your left, next door to Julia's of Wallingford and across Wallingford Ave. N from the Wallingford Center.

10.2   Continue by turning right (east) on N 44th St.

10.4   Left on Meridian Ave. N and cross N 45th St. Take the next right on N 46th St. and then again the next right on Bagley Ave. N. The Boulangerie is on the NE corner of N 45th St. and Bagley Ave. N.

10.5   Continue on ride by going back north on Bagley Ave. N., turning left on N 46th St. and right on Meridian Ave. N.

11.0   Cross N 55th St. The Honey Bear Bakery is straight ahead of you on the NE corner of the intersection.

11.0   Continue by going straight downhill on Kenwood Pl. N.

11.3   Right on E Green Lake Way N.

12.3   Left into Green Lake Community Center parking.

RIDE 7

DOWNTOWN DELIGHTS

This ride is designed to guide you on some alternate routes to and from downtown and to show you where to fulfill your sweet desires when you get there. While there are many bakeries to choose from downtown, I have tried to select a variety that illustrates the diversity of tastes available in the Puget Sound area.

GRAND CENTRAL BAKERY

Owner:	Gwenyth Basseti
Address:	214 1st Ave., Grand Central Arcade,
	Pioneer Square, Seattle
Phone:	622-3644
Hours:	Mon-Fri 7am-6pm; Sat-Sun 9am-5pm

Started in 1989, the Grand Central Bakery occupies the location of "the Bakery" begun in 1972, and has quickly become famous for its tremendous breads. Here you will find rich and chewy Italian-style breads with thick, hard crusts. Owner Gwenyth Basseti set out to produce this great bread after reading *The Italian Baker* by Carol Field, finding both an oven and a baker to get her started. The secret to Gwenyth's bread is careful duplication of the way it is made in Italy. Instead of the common yeast used as a bread starter, many of Grand Central's breads use "biga", which is Italian for "starter." The slow acting yeast creates a tasty and long lasting bread. It is baked in an oven that sprays water on top of each loaf, producing very hard crust and helps increase its shelf-life. That is not normally a problem for Grand Central breads. They are so authentic and delicious that many of the best Italian restaurants serve Grand Central bread where they quickly disappear.

The most famous bread for the Grand Central is their "como" bread, a sour dough Italian. Others include: wheat rye, yeasted cornmeal, focaccia and walnut. They also produce three types of sourdough breads: sour white, ciabatta and sour wheat. A different specialty bread is produced each day of the week. All breads are made by hand downstairs under the direction of head baker Leslie Mackie. In addition to breads, scones, soda bread, sticky buns, cakes, muffins, cookies and cinnamon rolls are very popular.

The window wall of bakery items at the Three Girls Bakery.

You will find ample indoor seating in a wonderful large atrium, outdoor seating on the rough cobbles of Pioneer Square, espresso, soups and sandwiches, cheeses and other Italian specialty items.

THREE GIRLS BAKERY

Owner:	Jack Levy
Address:	1514 Pike Place, Pike Place Market, Stall # 1, Seattle
Phone:	622-1045
Hours:	Mon-Sat 7am-6pm; **closed Sunday**

Jack Levy is very proud of the stall number for the Three Girls Bakery, Stall # 1, Pike Place Market. This business began in 1912 and, as the oldest continuous business in the market, gets the Stall # 1 designation under the seniority system. Jack has kept up the tradition for the last eight years.

The Three Girls is unusual in that it does not make its own products; it purchases them from a variety of bakeries throughout Seattle. This provides the customer with a very wide selection of breads, rolls and pastries. For example, the Three Girls stocks ten varieties of croissants and fourteen types of bagels. There are many cookies and muffins. For pure energy try the energy bar (whole wheat, dates, raisins, walnuts) or haystacks (chocolate covered coconut macaroon). Specialty breads include: onion poppy kuchon, cinnamon swirl and the huge Sicilian bread, a flat sourdough round.

The store is a glass wall of bread and pastry products, a wonderful visual way to display the variety. You can get really close and oogle each item, so close that you want to taste it. This is a great place to pick out some fresh bread to go with other products such as the cheeses you will find elsewhere in the Market. You will find an indoor sandwich counter, fast service and a wide variety of products.

PIROSHKY, PIROSHKY

Owners:	Zina and Vladimir Kotelnikov
Address:	1908 Pike Place, Pike Place Market, Seattle
Phone:	441-6068
Hours:	Mon-Sun 9am-5pm

Adding to the diversity of ethnic bakeries in the Puget Sound area is a new Russian bakery, Piroshky, Piroshky. "Piroshky" means "little surprise inside" in Russian, which is what you will find inside this very small space.

Zina and Vladimir Kotelnikov emigrated to the United States several years ago and, not too long after, opened their own bakery through opportunity, hard work and perseverance. Crammed in this tiny space, Vladimir turns out a constant stream of fresh baked goods right in front of your eyes. These are pastries you will not find anywhere else. You can watch him perform every step in baking and, if you are fluent in Russian, you can even talk with him while he works.

The pirsohkies come with different fillings, including: spiced mushroom and potato; mushroom, onion and celery; and rice and beef. You will also find baked apples encased in a thin dough and filled with honey, cheddar cheese

Unloading fresh loaves from the oven at Le Panier.

rolls, borscht, sauerkraut, vatrushka with apricot or sweet cheese, and a braid made of cinnamon, cardamom, raisins, orange peel and apples. There are drinks to accompany your pastry and a few stools inside where you can sit and watch Vladimir work.

LE PANIER VERY FRENCH BAKERY

Owner: Hubert Loevenbruck
Manager: Kimberly A. Wiganosky
Address: 1902 Pike Place, Pike Place Market, Seattle
Phone: 441-3669
Hours: Mon-Sat 7am-6:30pm; **closed Sunday**

The Pike Place Market is similar to the community markets of Europe, bustling with fresh produce and local people. Le Panier Very French Bakery fits well in this atmosphere, providing a taste of authentic French baking.

The bakery was started by Hubert Loevenbruck in 1983 to bring to the region an authentic French boulangerie. Originally from Normandy, France, Hubert felt that the same fine quality that was respected in France would be appreciated by Northwesterners. He imported a French stove, French supplies and French bakers to create the traditional bakery items. This attention to detail is demonstrated in the quality of all the products served.

For a special treat, arrive before 11:00 AM and you may get to see the bakers working at the French oven that is openly displayed. It is droolingly delightful to watch them prepare large loaves of spongy dough, deftly cutting the dough skin to let it expand during cooking. And it is even more delightful to watch the fresh baked loaves emerging from the oven, being stacked in baskets and made ready for your drooling lips.

The pastries are the traditional French style: croissant, almond croissant, chocolate croissant, choclatine (chocolate and almonds), friand (a butter rum crushed almond cookie), amandine (twice baked croissant with almond filling), meringue, palmier, charlotte citron (lemon mousse) and pear tart. These and other items are made fresh every day.

The breads are named after their shape and ingredients. These include: the very traditional baguette, epis (wheat), pain noix (nut), couronne (crown), son epis (whole wheat with oat top) and hazelnut. They also have feuilletes (square leaves of croissant dough filled with spinach, swiss cheese, broccoli or chicken). You will find espresso, coffee, hot chocolate, tea, cold drinks, milk, indoor seating and a bright modern interior.

A PIECE OF CAKE

Owner: Mr. Basil
Manager: Amy Luo
Address: 514 S King St., International District, Seattle
Phone: 623-8284
Hours: Mon-Fri 9am-7pm; Sat-Sun 10am-7pm

One of the attractions of Puget Sound is the diversity of nationalities living here. In the International District many bakeries demonstrate the interest of the Asian community in baked goods. One of them, A Piece of Cake, provides an alternative style bakery with a variety of French, Chinese and American pastries prepared by the head baker, Mr. Choung.

While cake may not be your first choice when you enter a bakery after bicycling, this is a good place to make an exception. The cake is very light, not too sugary and can be purchased by the slice. Flavors include: mango, napoleon, strawberry, mixed fruit, black forest, mandarin orange, chocolate cheesecake, amaretto cheesecake and French chestnut.

This bakery also has almond cookies (very light), coconut rolls, pork sausage rolls, filled steam buns, chicken pie, chocolate mousse, cream horns, sweet rolls, sponge cake, fruit tarts and swans (they look like swans). If you come here in September you can sample a unique treat, moon cakes. These are traditional gifts during the moon festival and are small cakes filled with very rich fillings. Do not be deceived by their size. It could take you several attempts to finish one.

You will find many new types of bakery products, inside seating, peach and mango soft drinks, International Examiner and Asia Today newspapers and Seattle's Best Coffee coffee.

TIO'S BAKERY AND CAFE

Owner: Carlos Penhuela
Address: 2379 Eastlake Ave. E, Eastlake Neighborhood, Seattle
Phone: 325-0081
Hours: Mon-Thurs 7am-7pm; Fri-Sat 7am-Midnight;
Sun 8am-4pm

The Eastlake Neighborhood of Seattle is an eclectic area of houseboats, small businesses and cramped apartments, cut off from the rest of Seattle by Interstate 5. Tio's Bakery and Cafe, a funky eatery, fits right in this environment. For many, it provides a place to hang out and eat great bakery products in a relaxed atmosphere. For others, it is a convenient stop on a popular bicycle commuting route, where they can pick up a pastry on their way to work.

The bakery products are of the whole wheat variety and there are many unusual items. Large, thick lemon bars, whole wheat spice cookies, cinnamon rolls made from brioche dough, fresh peach danish, cheese croissants, and plump bagels with various fruit fillings. Chief baker Claude Juillauma's French origins are evident in the variety of French styled baked goods such as the brioche and croissants. He also prepares fancy cakes that are not all chocolate. There are also more American items such as large Mazurka bars, apricot bars, honey-nut bars, whole wheat cinnamon rolls and many types of large cookies.

The ambiance is sunny and funky. There are several sofas located around the very large seating area, two walls are mostly windows, providing a great amount of light, and tables of all sizes and shapes.There are even wooden high chairs for any mini-bicyclists you may bring along. In addition to bakery products, there are breakfast, lunch and dinner items, expresso, coffee, tea, fresh squeezed orange juice and lemonade, and hot cider. You will find a bike rack outside, restrooms and plenty of places to sit and relax.

THE RIDES

The idea behind this ride is to suggest several reasonable routes into and out of downtown from North Seattle. When ridden on a weekend morning, the traffic is usually not very heavy.

Special Note: Please carry and use your bike lock on this trip. The Elliott Bay Bicycle Shop is located two blocks north of the Pike Place Market at 2116 Western Ave. Ti Cycles is located just east of Western Ave. at 824 Post Alley off of Marion St.

BALLARD ROUTE

Start: Hiram M. Chittenden Locks, Ballard Neighborhood, Seattle

Miles: 14.7

Difficulty: Easy. Some traffic

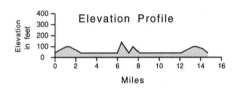

0.0   Start this ride at Chittenden Locks in Ballard. To get there, from I-5 take exit 169 and turn west on NE 45th St. Follow NE 45th St. into Ballard where it becomes Market St. Stay on Market St. and the locks are 0.5 miles west of downtown Ballard on your left. You are **not** allowed to ride your bicycle in the U.S. Corp of Engineers "project" (minimum $25 federal fine), so please walk from the front entrance to the gray building. Cross the lock gates on a narrow steel plated walkway to the south side.

0.3   Left on W Commodore Way.

1.1   Right on 24th Ave. W.

1.3   Right onto a pedestrian/bicycle bridge over the railroad tracks at the corner of W Elmore St. and 24th Ave. W.

1.4   Left on Gilman Ave. W.

2.2   Straight on 20th Ave. W. The sign is not easily seen. When Thorndyke angles right and uphill, continue straight and down a gentle grade to the railroad yards.

2.5   Left at cyclone fence on the Pier 91 Bikeway. The bikeway to the right goes to Chandlers Cove but you cannot get downtown that way. Take the bikeway on the left (east) side.

3.3   Make a hard right across the road onto the sidewalk next to the water. This is the Elliott Bay Bicycle Path extension. Follow the path marked for wheels to the south end of Myrtle Edwards Park.

4.9   Leave Myrtle Edwards Park and go south through parking lot to Alaskan Way.

5.0   Straight on Alaskan Way. The road is rough in places and there are several railroad track crossings.

Vladimir Kotelnikov baking at Piroshky, Piroshky.

5.5   Left at Lenora St. sign under the concrete roadway that goes over Alaskan Way and ends out over the water. Enter the Seattle Waterfront Pathway and continue south along waterfront, past the Pike Place Market on your left.

6.0   Left on University St. and left again on Western Ave., to double back to the Market.

6.4   Right at top of hill onto Pike Place and the Market. CAUTION! The cobblestones can be very slippery when wet or at low speeds. You will find Piroshky Piroshky, Le Panier Very French Bakery and the Three Girls Bakery along Pike Place on your left.

6.4   Leave the Pike Place Market at the north end and head back down Western Ave.

7.1   Left on Yesler Way and right on 1st Ave. Left at the next street, Washington St., to Occidental Park. Walk your bicycle across the huge cobblestones to the southwest corner of the square where you will see the entrance to the Grand Central Arcade and the Grand Central Bakery.

7.2   Return to Washington St. and head east.

7.5   Right on 5th Ave.

7.9   Left on King St., the first street past the light at Jackson St. A Piece of Cake is on your left in the middle of the block.

THE RETURN

7.9   Leave A Piece of Cake and head east to 6th Ave. S and turn left. Go one block to Jackson St. and turn left at the light. Continue straight west on Jackson St. to Alaskan Way.

8.2   Right on Seattle Waterfront Pathway just before Alaskan Way and behind the "Do Not Enter" sign. Follow this north to the end.

9.2   Right on Alaskan Way.

9.7   Straight into parking lot to Myrtle Edwards Park. Retrace your route along the bikepaths.

12.6 Right (straight) on 20th Ave. W which turns into Gilman Ave. W.

13.3 Right on W Emerson Pl. and immediately left on 23rd Ave. W.

13.5 Left on W Commodore Way.

14.2 Right into Commodore Park. Remember to walk your bicycle when you enter the "project."

14.7 Entrance to Hiram M. Chittenden Locks.

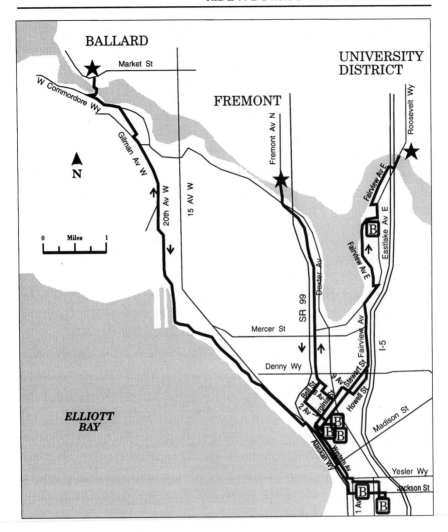

FREMONT ROUTE

Start: Fremont Bridge, Fremont Neighborhood, Seattle

Miles: 8.8

Difficulty: Moderate. Some hills, some traffic.

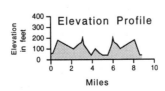

0.0   Start at the north end of the Fremont Bridge in Fremont. Cross the bridge on the right hand sidewalk. On the south side of the bridge re-enter the street very carefully -- there are a lot of cars that turn right onto Florentia St. and there is poor visiblity.

0.2   Get in right lane next to curb and go across intersection at a slight left angle onto Dexter Ave. N. There is a moderate hill up Dexter.

1.7   Cross Mercer St.

2.1   Cross Denny Way.

2.2   Right on Bell St.

2.5   Left on 2nd Ave. Get into right lane.

2.8   Right on Stewart St.

3.0   Pike Place.

3.2   Leave the Pike Place Market at the north end and turn left on Virgina St. and immediately left on Western Ave.

3.9   Left on Yesler Way and right on 1st Ave. Then next left, Washington St., to Occidental Park. Walk your bicycle across the huge cobblestones to the southwest corner of the square where you will see the entrance to the Grand Central Arcade and the Grand Central Bakery.

4.0   Return to Washington St. and head east.

4.3   Right on 5th Ave.

4.7   Left on King St., the first street past the light at Jackson St. A Piece of Cake is on your left in the middle of the block.

THE RETURN

4.7   Leave A Piece of Cake and head east to 6th Ave. S and turn left. Go one block to Jackson St. and turn left at the light. Continue straight west on Jackson St. to Alaskan Way.

5.0   Right underneath the Alaskan Viaduct. Continue north to University St.

5.5   Right on University St. and then left on Western Ave.

5.9   Right on Virginia St. This is an extremely steep street. Do not be embarassed to walk up the sidewalk.

6.1   Left on 6th Ave.

6.2   Right on Blanchard St.

6.25   Left on 7th Ave.

6.4   Cross Denny Way.

6.7   Cross Mercer St.

8.6   Straight across Fremont Bridge. There is a small ramp up to the sidewalk 100' before the bridge. Use it. The bridge deck is steel grating and not safe to ride on.

8.8   North side of Fremont Bridge.

UNIVERSITY ROUTE

Start: University Bridge, University District, Seattle

Miles: 11.0

Difficulty: Moderate. Some traffic.

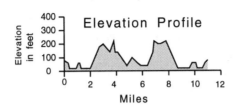

0.0   Start at north end of University Bridge on Roosevelt Way. Keep in far right lane which is a bike lane.

0.3   Right on Fuhrman Ave. E immediately upon crossing bridge.

0.4   Left on Fairview Ave. E.

0.7   Left on E Hamlin St. This is a very steep uphill. Walk, if necessary.

0.8   Right on Eastlake Ave. E.

1.0   Right on E Roanoke St. Tio's Bakery is one block south on Eastlake Ave. E.

1.1   Continue left on Fairview Ave. E.

1.7   Pass tiny Terry Pettus Park with access to the water.

1.8   Left on E Garfield St.

1.9   Right on Eastlake Ave E. and get in left lane.

2.0   Straight through light on Eastlake Ave E.

3.0   Right on Stewart St. It is a straight road to the market.

3.9   Pike Place Market. Le Panier is on the right corner.

4.1   Leave the Pike Place Market at the north end and turn left on Virgina St. and immediately left on Western Ave.

4.8   Left on Yesler Way and right on 1st Ave. Left at the next street, Washington St., to Occidental Park. Walk your bicycle across the huge cobblestones to the southwest corner of the square where you will see the entrance to the Grand Central Arcade and the Grand Central Bakery.

4.9   Return to Washington St. and head east.

5.2   Right on 5th Ave.

5.6   Left on King St., the first street past the light at Jackson St. A Piece of Cake is on your left in the middle of the block.

THE RETURN

5.6   Leave A Piece of Cake and head east to 6th Ave. S and turn left. Go one block to Jackson St. and turn left at the light. Continue straight west on Jackson St. to Alaskan Way.

5.9   Right underneath the Alaskan Viaduct. Continue north to University St.

6.4   Right on University St. and then left on Western Ave.

6.8   Right on Virginia St. This is an extremely steep street. Do not be embarassed to walk up the sidewalk.

7.2   Right on 9th Ave.

7.3   Left on Howell St. which angles left at the freeway.

7.8   Cross Stewart St. The road you are on becomes Eastlake Ave. E.

8.7   Continue straight on Eastlake Ave. E.

8.8   Left on E. Garfield St.

8.9   Right on Fairview Ave. E.

9.6   Right on E Roanoke St. This is a steep uphill.

9.8   Left on Eastlake Ave. E.

10.1   Left on E Hamlin St.

10.2   Right on Fairview Ave. E.

10.6   Continue right on Fuhrman Ave. E.

10.7   Left on Eastlake Ave. E. and cross University Bridge.

11.0   North side of University Bridge.

RIDE 8

LAKE WASHINGTON BOULEVARD

Since the turn of the century, the "Boulevard" has been a favorite
bike route for local bicyclists. It is one of the flattest roads around
of any distance and provides outstanding views, numerous parks
and is closed to motor vehicles several Saturdays and Sundays in
the summer.

DAILY GRIND

Owner: Jackson Cremer
Address: 2301 24th Ave. E, Montlake Neighborhood, Seattle
Phone: 322-9885
Hours: Mon-Sun 4am-2pm

Do you like to get started early in the morning? The Daily Grind is the
place for you. Open at four AM! Bring your lights!

This is a cozy little neighborhood breakfast place with outrageous
scones and muffins baked on the premises. The baked goods are limited in
variety but not in size, texture or taste. The whole wheat scones are raisin,
apple walnut, cranberry orange, banana raspberry and apple blueberry. The
white scones are honey-date nut, peach, orange and mixed berry. These scones
are not the common orderly triangular shaped smoothies. These are large wild-
shaped monsters. The muffins are just as wild looking and just as good. For a
change of pace, you can buy the scone and muffin mixes to try out yourself.

The Daily Grind also bakes cinnamon rolls, but these too, are a bit
different from what you will find elsewhere. They are not made with raised
dough, are not too sweet and have plenty of cinnamon. The combination is
both different and delicious.

In addition to baked goods, The Daily Grind serves breakfast and lunch
items. You will find plenty of seating, restrooms, a casual atmosphere, soft
drinks and espresso, including the "Jackson" (mocha and almond) named
after the proprietor. The regular customers keep their personal latte discount
cards posted right next to the checkout counter.

EXQUISITE DESSERTS

Owners: Debby Egger and Patty Sullivan
Address: 2800 E Madison St., Madison Neighborhood, Seattle
Phone: 328-0518
Hours: Mon-Fri 7:30am-6pm, Sat-Sun 8:30am-5pm

Interested in great tasting baked goods? Interested in healthy baked goods? This is the place for you. Debby and Patty have spent years creating baked goods without sugar that are both healthy and look and taste great.

Patty Sullivan started baking for two children who were hyperglycemic and her baking was appreciated by others. Like good dough, the idea and the demand just continued to grow resulting in the creation of Exquisite Desserts. Obviously, their products are popular with diabetics and others who need to be careful about their intake of sugar, but many customers come for the delicious flavors first and consider the healthy ingredients a nice plus.

Most recently, Debby and Patty have been working on products that are both sugar free and have no added oil. These new products include: scones, muffins, biscotti, brownies, chocolate cake, banana bars and cookies. In some ways every item in this store is a specialty.

If you are looking for a balanced diet, try their fresh turkey sandwiches prepared every day, popular with the regular lunch group. You will also find espresso, coffee, day olds, deli sandwiches and soups. The Exquisite Desserts products can also be found in some area supermarkets.

STOLL'S MADISON PARK BAKERY

Owner: Fred Stoll
Address: 4214 E Madison St.,
Madison Park Neighborhood, Seattle
Phone: 322-3238
Hours: Tues-Fri 7am-6:30pm; Sat 7am-5:30pm;
closed Sunday and Monday

Stoll's Madison Park Bakery is a traditional, full-line bakery in the heart of old Madison Park. Fred Stoll learned the baker's trade from his father who took over this bakery from Ben Opperminer in 1945, who originally started it in 1929. Although German by ancestry, most of Fred's bakery items are the more popular traditional American styles. Here you will find a wide selection of items with plenty of sugar, displayed in five glass display cases. Choose

Early morning along Lake Washington.

from hopscotch bars (chocolate chips, butterscotch chips, coconut, white chocolate chips), matinee cookies (chocolate cookie with white chocolate chips), Nanaimo bars, tarts, eclairs, cream cakes, donuts, maple bars, white wheat frosted cinnamon rolls, danish, honey-nut coffee cakes, French twists and raspberry coffee cake (strips).

Specialties include: Scottish shortbread (from an old Scottish recipe handed down), caramel twists, Ozark bread (French bread with cornmeal on top) and pecan cups (small roll-ups with a pecan glazed topping). There is usually one entire case devoted to cookies, both the large variety and small ones, such as pralines, thumbprints, raisin oatmeal, trail mix (peanuts, raisins, chocolate chips, coconut), butter lemon bars and dutch girls (bread dough rolled thin with a light sugar glaze). There is always a variety of pies, cakes and bundt cakes in both 8" and 6" sizes, small enough for a hungry cyclist.

You will find five tables inside, self-service espresso and Caffe Mauro coffee. There is ample space for bicycles on the wide sidewalk outside. If the weather is nice, take a short walk (ride) east and stretch out on the grass at Madison Park.

PERT'S, A DELI ON LESHI

Owners: Sue Pert and Gaye Ishimaru
Address: 120 Lakeside Ave., Leschi Neighborhood, Seattle
Phone: 325-0277
Hours: Mon-Sat 8am-4pm, Sun 8am-2pm

Pert's is located on one of the most popular bicycle routes in the city of Seattle along the western shore of Lake Washington. The area of Leshi was once the terminus of a ferry that operated over to Mercer Island. Now it is home to a few upscale business establishments, including Pert's. Although relatively new to the area, it is fast becoming the place to hang out.

The head baker, Karen Baler, produces Seattle's favorite baked goods - scones, muffins, bars and cream coffee cake. The scones are very large and some have gooey fruit fillings. These scones were once voted Seattle's Best scones by Seattle Weekly readers. You will also find sesame oat rolls, cinnamon twists and a variety of sheet bars.

Breads include banana walnut and orange pecan. Cookies include oatmeal, chocolate chip and peanut butter. Karen also makes sugar free bran muffins and soda biscuits. On weekends, Pert's prepares large sticky cinnamon rolls that are popular with bicyclists.

In addition to baked products there is a full range of lunch deli items including sandwiches, pasta salad, beer, wine and a variety of soft drinks, including Snapple drinks. You will find ample seating both inside and out, a bright interior, restrooms and a counter looking out on Lakeside Ave. Just north on Lakeside Ave. is Il Vechi's (the Old Man's), a bike shop run by George Gibbs, an original Squadro Porcello team member (see Preface).

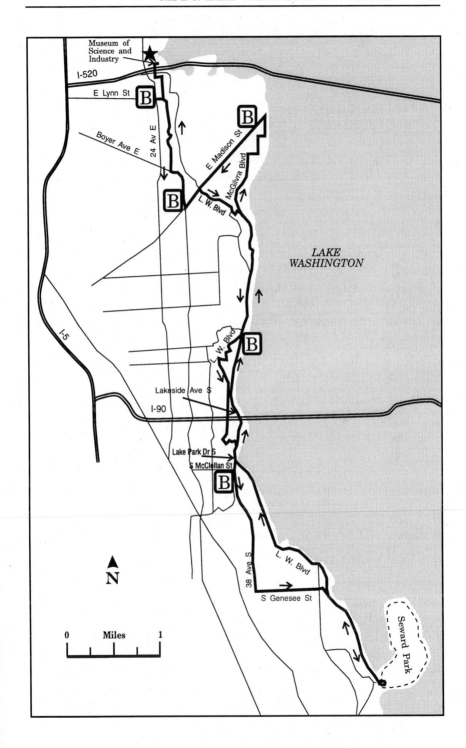

BAKER'S BEACH CAFE

Owners: Patience Cryst and Lenard Yen
Address: 3601 S McClellan St.,
   Mt. Baker Neighborhood, Seattle
Phone: 725-3654
Hours: Mon-Fri 6:30am-9pm; Sat-Sun 7am-3pm

Nestled in a quiet old neighborhood called Mt. Baker is a new cafe with wonderful baked goods. The atmosphere is relaxed, where you will find everyone from families with children to hungry cyclists.

Baker's Beach was started by Patience Cryst and Lenard Yen as a place for good food in a very casual atmosphere. Trained as a bakery chef and experienced in larger establishments, Patience now brings her skills to this lucky neighborhood. In the tiny kitchen in back, she turns out a great variety of tempting baked products, which include: big, rich bars, pies, coffee cakes and cookies. If you are looking for energy try the large seven layer bar, white chocolate brownie or cheesecake. Patience also produces carrot cake, currant scones, almond coffee cake, peanut butter bars, lemon bars and monster muffins. The large raspberry scones are tremendous, dusted with a heavy layer of powdered sugar. In addition, they have bagels and hot pasta, quiche, lasagna and pizza.

At Baker's Beach, you will find casual inside seating where you can enjoy a meal of baked goods or a full breakfast or lunch entree. They serve espresso, coffee and assorted soft drinks to accompany your food. You will also find restrooms and a bike rack.

THE RIDE

This is a variation on one of the most popular bike rides in Seattle, Lake Washington Boulevard. You will go on back roads through the hilly Harrison neighborhood, climb along old scenic roads above Lake Washington and return along the shores of Lake Washington.

Start: Museum of Science and Industry, Montlake Neighborhood, Seattle. From I-5, take the I-520 exit 168. From I-520 take the Montlake exit and continue straight across Montlake Pl. E. Take the next left on 24th Ave. E. Park in the large parking lot of the Museum.

Miles: 19.7

Difficulty: Moderate. Some hills

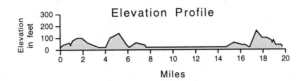

Elevation Profile

0.0   Start at Museum of Science and Industry. Head south on 24th Ave. E.

0.1   Cross E Lake Washington Blvd. Follow the bike route signs for the Lake Washington Loop to Seward Park.

0.15 Left into alley.

0.2   Right on Glenwilde Pl. E.

0.3   Left on E Roanoke St.

0.35 Right on 25th Ave. E.

0.5   Cross E Lynn St. The Daily Grind is located one block to your right (west) at E Lynn St. and 24th Ave. E. The Montlake Bicycle Shop is located to the south across E Lynn St.

0.8   Left on Boyer Ave. E (unmarked) where 25th Ave. E ends at a "T" with a traffic circle.

0.9   Right on 26th Ave. E.

1.1   Left on E Galer St.

1.2   Right on 26th Ave. E.

1.5   Angle right on 28th Ave. E.

1.9   Left on E Madison St. Exquisite Desserts is located on your left at the northeast corner of 28th Ave. E and E Madison St.

2.0   Right on Lake Washington Boulevard.

2.8   Pass Denny Blaine Park on your left with water access.

3.4   Continue straight on Lake Washington Boulevard.

4.0   Right uphill on Lake Washington Boulevard. Pert's Deli is on your left at 120 Lakeside Ave.

4.4   Continue straight on Lake Washington Boulevard. CAUTION! The cross traffic does not have to stop.

5.2   I-90 bridge viewpoint on left. Ride 10 describes the route across the bridge and Mercer Island to Bellevue.

5.9   Right on Lake Washington Boulevard.

6.1   Right on Lake Park Drive S.

6.4   Left on McClellan. Bakers Beach is straight ahead to your right.

6.7   Straight on Hunter Blvd. S.

7.0   Continue straight on 38th Ave. S.

7.5   Left on S Genesse St.

8.1   Continue straight on S Genesse.

8.2   Angle right downhill on short road going down to
       Lake Washington Boulevard.

8.3   Right on Lake Washington Boulevard.

9.4   Left into Seward Park where there are restrooms. For a nice extension
       to this ride, ride around the Seward Park peninsula. It is about 3 miles,
       right on the water, with no cars. Take your time and enjoy the serenity
       available by bicycle here in the midst of a large metropolitan area.

THE RETURN

9.6   Right onto Lake Washington Boulevard.

14.0   Pert's Deli is on your right.

14.7   Continue straight on Lake Washington Boulevard.

15.4   Right on McGilvra Blvd. E.

16.1   Right on E Lee St.

16.3   Left on 42nd Ave. E.

16.4   Right on E Garfield St.

16.45 Left on 43rd Ave. E.

16.7   Left on E Madison St.

16.8   Stoll's Madison Park Bakery is on the right at 4214 E Madison.
       Continue west on E Madison St. up and over a long hill.

17.9   Right on 28th Ave. E. Angle left up hill.

18.7   Right on 26th Ave. E.

18.8   Left on Boyer Ave. E.

18.9   Right at next street, 25th Ave. E. (unmarked).

19.2   Continue straight on 25th Ave. E. The Daily Grind is located one block
       to your left (west) at E Lynn St. and 24th Ave. E.

19.5   Left on E Roanoke St.

19.55 Right on Glenwilde Pl. E and immediately left into alley.

19.6   Right following Lake Washington Loop signs.

19.6   Cross I-520 on 24th Ave. E.

19.7   Museum of History and Industry.

RIDE 9

EDMONDS BY BACKROADS

A reasonable bicycling distance north of Seattle via back roads, Edmonds has long been a mecca for cyclists. It remains a little community that has not lost its charm in spite of all of the growth taking place elsewhere. This ride will take you to one of the main attractions in Edmonds, Brusseau's.

BRUSSEAU'S

Owner: William Keegan
Address: 115 5th Ave. S, Edmonds
Phone: 774-4166
Hours: Mon-Fri 7am-5pm; Sat-Sun 8am-5pm

Brusseau's in Edmonds is a wonderful bakery with a European touch. It is fancy but not pretentious, attractive and tastful and, as an added attraction, it has a large outdoor patio that permits bicyclists to stay close to their beloved bicycles while they eat.

Brusseau's was started by Jerlyn Brusseau back in 1978. William Keegan baked for Jerlyn for several years and then took over the ownership in 1992. Many of the products are his creations. For example, the wonderful bread pudding served in a glass mug is his mother's recipe for using leftovers from baking.

You will find a variety of offerings: from cinnamon rolls to cheeses, teas to champagne. Breakfast and lunch items, wine and espresso are also available. Careful attention is given to making products healthy, using organically grown ingredients where possible. For example, there is no oil in the granola and no preservatives in any products.

You will find fancy inside tables, restrooms, espresso and a large outdoor area with picnic tables. Squadro Porcello (see Preface) has been visiting Brusseau's since it first opened in 1978 and even had birthday jerseys made in honor of Brusseau's 10th anniversary. Once you discover this wonderful bakery, it will become a regular bicycle destination for you, too.

THE RIDE

This is a great ride, perfect for really getting in shape, but it can be strenuous for those just starting out. The out-and-back route has some small differences going each way. Follow directions carefully until you get the route down. The elevation profile is the same and therefore is only shown between the starting and ending points.

Start: Lower Woodland Park, Green Lake Neighborhood, Seattle. From I-5, take the NE 45th St. exit 169. Go west along NE 45th St. and turn right on Stone Way N which becomes Green Lake Way N. Follow Green Lake Way N and you will see a large parking area parallel to you on the left with play fields behind it. Park in this parking lot.

Miles: 27.3

Difficulty: Moderate. Some big hills and busy street crossings.

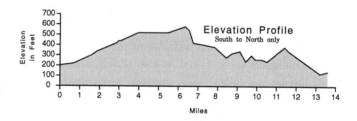

0.0   Start at Lower Woodland Park in the parking area next to the baseball and soccer fields. Head out the north end of the parking lot and turn left on W Green Lake Ave. N.

0.5   Left on N 63rd St. under Aurora. This is not marked but it is the second left that is paved.

0.7   Continue in right lane on Linden Ave. N.

0.9   Left on N 67th St.

1.0   Right on Fremont Ave. N.

1.6   Cross N 80th St.

1.9   Cross N 85th St. CAUTION! Heavy traffic. You can activate the pedestrian signal light crossing to stop the traffic.

2.9   Cross N 105th St. CAUTION! Heavy traffic.

3.0   Left on N 107th St. There is a windmill park to your left.

3.1   Right on Evanston Ave. N.

4.0   Cross N 125th St. CAUTION! Poor visibility both directions.

4.2   Right on N 130th St.

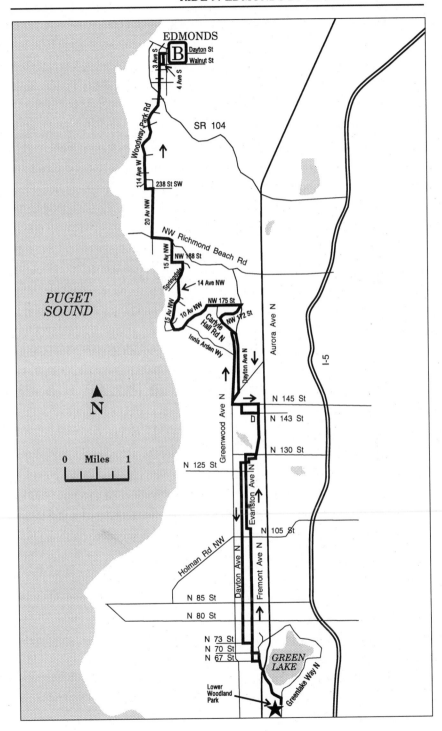

4.4   Left on Linden Ave. N. at light at bottom of hill. Bitter Lake Park is on your left.

5.0   Left on N 143rd St.

5.3   Right on Dayton Ave. N (a big pine tree hides this sign).

5.4   Left on N 145th St. This road has high speed traffic, so get into right lane immediately.

5.5   Right on Greenwood Ave. N. Immediately get in left turn lane and continue north on Greenwood Ave. N.

6.3   Continue straight on Greenwood Ave. N and begin descent of a very steep hill with a "T" intersection at the bottom.

6.7   Left on Carlyle Hall Rd. N.

6.9   Veer right onto NW 172nd St.

7.4   Left on N 175th St.

7.9   Left on 10th Ave. NW which winds downhill and then uphill.

8.7   Viewpoint on left. Please stop off the paved surface. To the north you can see the community of Richmond Beach.

9.1   Continue left on 14th Ave. NW. This will take you to the top of another steep hill.

9.4   Right on Springdale Ct. NW at bottom of steep hill. CAUTION! There are several steel plates in the middle of the roadway at this intersection with holes around them. Do not ride on them if it is wet.

9.7   Left on NW 188th St.

9.9   Right on 15th Ave. NW.

10.2   Left on NW Richmond Beach Rd.

10.5   Right on 20th Ave. NW.

11.4   Left on 238th St. SW.

11.6   Right on 114th Ave. W. Note that the speed limit in the town of Woodway, which you are in, is 25 mph. You may exceed this going down the hill into Edmonds.

13.5   Right on Dayton St.

13.6   Brusseau's in Edmonds is located on the northeast corner of Dayton St. and 5th Ave.

THE RETURN

13.6   Leave Brusseau's and head back (west) on Dayton St.

13.7   Left on 4th Ave.

13.8   Right on Walnut St.

13.8   Left on 3rd Ave. S, which becomes Woodway Park Rd. (unmarked).

15.7   Left on 238th St. SW.

15.8 Right on Timber Lane.

16.7 Left on NW 195th St. (NW Richmond Beach Rd.)

17.0 Right on 15th Ave. W.

17.3 Left on NW 188th St.

17.5 Right on Springdale Ct. NW.

17.8 Continue left following big yellow arrow (<) uphill on 14th Ave. NW.

18.1 Continue right on 15th Ave. NW.

19.3 Right on NW 175th St.

19.9 Right on Greenwood Pl. N.

20.3 Left on Carlyle Hall Rd.

20.6 Right on Dayton Ave. N.

21.5 Right on Westminster Way N.

21.8 Left on N 145th St.

22.1 Right on Linden Ave. N.

22.9 Cross N 130th St.

23.0 Right on N 129th St.

23.1 Left on Fremont Ave. N.

23.15 Right on N 127th St.

23.2 Left on Dayton Ave. N.

23.4 Cross N 125th St.

26.0 Left on N 73rd St.

26.1 Right on Fremont Ave. N.

26.3 Left on N 70th St.

26.4 Right on Linden Ave. N. Left under Aurora, then right along W Green Lake Way N.

27.3 Right into parking lot at Lower Woodland Park.

RIDE 10

LAKE WASHINGTON LOOP

One of the great longer rides in this area is the ride around Lake Washington. In the old days, this required a 60 mile ride along somewhat dangerous roads. Nowadays, the route is shortened and safer with the addition of many miles of bicycle paths. The route I have chosen for this book crosses Lake Washington on the I-90 floating bridge bike path which now extends across Mercer Island. This shortens the ride and prevents having to wander through Renton and trying to survive Rainier Ave. S. This is still a good workout which includes going over Juanita Hill, a better alternative than the four lane road going north to Bothell from Juanita. The route passes several bakeries already described, including: the Daily Grind (Ride 8), Pert's Deli (Ride 8), Great Harvest Bread Company (Ride 4) and A La Francaise (Ride 4). Two more bakeries are introduced along the way. You don't have to, but you could eat at every bakery. Start early in the day.

FRENCH PASTRY PLACE, LTD.

Owners: Jean-Claude Ferre and LeeAnn Belarde
Address: 7695 SE 27th St., Mercer Island
Phone: 236-1727
Hours: Mon-Thurs 7am-6:30pm; Fri 7am-7pm;
Sat 8am-5pm; Sun 8am-3pm

This new bakery is run by Jean-Claude Ferre, a Frenchman trained in France in the art of French baking. He and his partner, LeeAnn Belarde, have made The French Pastry Place a bright, cheerful bakery where quality is the key ingredient. If you close your eyes while you take a bite of one of their fresh croissants, you may believe for a moment that you're in Paris.

The French baked goods are all very beautiful as well as wonderful tasting. Croissants are presented either plain, with almond paste and almonds, with ham and cheese or as the holders for turkey, roast beef, egg salad or tuna sandwiches. The croissants even go into the delicious bread pudding. You will also enjoy fruit tarts year round, diamond-molded chocolates, chocolate dipped cookies, bear claws made from croissant dough, lemon cake with fresh lemons, pecan tarts, swan's with fresh whipped cream, and a cappuccino roll. They also have several types of French breads including batard, epis petite, country loaf and the traditional baguette.

You will find many drinks including Torrefazione coffee and espresso, Snapple and Koala sodas, Perrier, and fresh apple and orange juices. There are ample tables inside and restrooms. The tiled floor is pretty, but be careful with cleats.

Jean-Claude Ferre and Lee Anne Belard of the French Pastry Place.

CRAWFORD'S BAKERY CAFE COMPANY

Owners: Michael and Alexis Petrone
Address: 10246A Main St., Bellevue
Phone: 451-3761
Hours: Mon-Sat 7am-6pm; Sun 7am-1pm

Tucked into the old Bellevue downtown is a new bakery run by a young couple from back East. Michael and Alexis Petrone have brought with them their baking skills and an array of products more commonly seen on the east coast, which Michael and Alexis have quickly adapted to the tastes of their Northwest customers.

Michael makes all of the bakery products from scratch except the bagels, which are provided by Spot Bagel. You will find many types of large muffins, large cookies and large sheet bars. For those with a demanding sweet tooth, try the large coconut mounds or a Sarah Burnhardt cookie (Amaretto cookie with chocolate mousse and hot chocolate covering). The scones are made with buttermilk giving them a slight tang. They make their own granola and croutons.

Italian sodas, soft drinks, Caffe Mauro espresso and coffee are available to accompany the large servings. You will enjoy the bright, airy seating area. Make sure to visit the restrooms before you get on your way again, because you will get to pass by the kitchen where you can see the hustle and bustle of treats in production.

THE RIDE

This is a fairly challenging ride in terms of length, hills and traffic. Your reward is great views, some fun roads to ride and the accomplishment of riding around a large part of Lake Washington.

Start: Museum of Science and Industry, Montlake Neighborhood, Seattle. From I-5, take the I-520 exit 168. From I-520 take the Montlake exit and continue straight across Montlake Pl. E. Take the next left on 24th Ave. E. Park in the large parking lot of the Museum of Science and Industry.

Miles: 39.6

Difficulty: Difficult. Long steep hills, traffic and distance.

0.0   Start at Museum of Science and Industry. Head south on 24th Ave E.

0.1   Cross E Lake Washington Blvd. Follow the bike route signs for the Lake Washington Loop to Seward Park.

NOTE: For a more detailed map of the start, see the map for Ride 8: Lake Washington Boulevard. Directions diverge at mile 5.2.

0.15   Left into alley.

0.2   Right on Glenwilde Pl. E.

0.3   Left on E Roanoke St.

0.35   Right on 25th Ave. E.

0.5   Cross E Lynn St. The Daily Grind (See Ride 8) is located one block to your right (west) at E Lynn St. and 24th Ave. E.

0.8   Left on E Boyer Ave. (unmarked).

0.9   Right on 26th Ave. E.

1.1   Left on E Galer St.

1.2   Right on 27th Ave. E.

1.5   Angle right on 28th Ave. E.

1.9   Left on E Madison St. Exquisite Desserts (See Ride 8) is located on your left at the northeast corner of 28th Ave. E and E Madison St.

2.0   Right on Lake Washington Blvd.

2.8   Pass Denny Blaine Park on your left with water access.

4.0   Right uphill on Lake Washington Boulevard. Pert's Deli (See Ride 8) is on your left in shopping area.

4.4   Continue straight on Lake Washington Boulevard. CAUTION! The cross traffic does not have to stop.

4.6   Frink Park on left.

5.2   Turn left on S Irving and take immediate right onto the bike path going downhill onto I-90 bridge.

6.9   Exit bridge and go straight uphill, turn left and keep right on path.

7.1   Cross Mercer Way, turn left onto the sidewalk and then keep right up and over the hill.

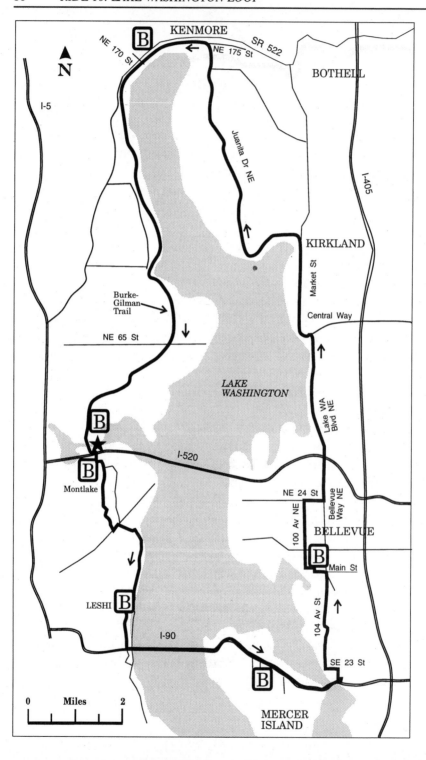

7.7   Cross 76th St. SE.

7.9   Cross 77th St. SE. To visit the French Pastry Place, turn right on 77th St. SE and go one block (south). The bakery is on the corner of 77th St. SE and SE 27th St. Return via the same route to get back on the bike path. Continue east along bike paths on north side of I-90.

NOTE: For a more complete map, call Region 1 of the Washington State Department of Transportation and request a map of the I-90 bike path.

10.3   Exit I-90 bike path at SE 34th St. and 109th Ave. NE.

10.3   Left on SE 34th St., then right on 108th Ave. SE.

11.0   Left on SE 23rd St., then right on 104th Ave. SE.

12.1   Right on SE 10th St. to Bellevue Way, then left on Bellevue Way.

13.0   Left on Main St.

13.1   Crawford's Bakery is on your right at 10246A Main St.

13.2   To continue, turn right onto 102nd Ave. NE, then left on NE 1st St.

13.3   Right on 100th Ave. NE.

14.8   Right on NE 24th St.

15.1   Left on Bellevue Way NE.

15.7   Cross over I-520.

16.8   Continue left on Lake Washington Blvd. NE.

18.2   Turn left on Central Way, then right onto Market St.

20.3   Left onto Juanita Dr. NE.

26.1   Turn left onto NE 175th St.

26.9   Enter Tracey Owen Station Park.

27.7   Cross NE 170th St. The Great Harvest Bread Company is to your right in the shopping center at the back (see Ride 4).

31.7   Matthews Beach is on your left (unmarked) before bridge crossing over Sand Point Way NE. Restrooms and access to Lake Washington.

37.4   Cross 30th Ave. NE. Exit here to go to A La Francaise (see Ride 4).

38.6   Turn off Burke-Gilman at Hec Edmundson Pavilion. There is an old, concrete pedestrian/bike bridge over Montlake Blvd. Carefully go down ramp and stay on sidewalk on east side of Montlake Blvd. Cross Montlake Bridge and go across E Shelby St. staying on sidewalk on east side of Montlake Blvd.

39.5   Left on E Hamlin St. At the bottom of the hill turn right and pass through the gap in the concrete barrier, make a U turn to get to the parking lot of the Museum of Science and Industry.

39.6   Museum of Science and Industry.

COUNTRY BAKERIES

Bainbridge Bakery
Black Diamond Bakery
Bob's Bakery
Calico Cupboard, The
City Bakery
Country Bakery, The
George's Bakery
Langley Village Bakery
Oosterwyk's Dutch Bakery
The Original Bakery
Original Brown Bag Cafe and Bakery,The
Rainier Natural Food Store and Bakery
Scandia Bakery and Lefse Factory
Sky River Bakery
Sluys Poulsbo Bakery
Sultan Bakery
Sweet Life Cafe

COUNTRY RIDES

Mark, Laurie and Melissa on the Enumclaw Plateau.

RIDE 11

CARNATION COUNTRY CAPER

The Carnation Valley, or lower Snoqualmie Valley, is a great place
to bicycle. It is a flat place with aromatic farms and scenic views.
This ride takes you from Fall City to the small, but growing,
community of Carnation. You will wander through the back roads,
along and over the Snoqualmie and Tolt Rivers and return via the
same, easy route.

THE ORIGINAL BROWN BAG CAFE AND BAKERY

Owner:	Alex Awasthi
Address:	4366 Tolt Ave., Carnation
Phone:	333-6100
Hours:	Mon-Sun 6:30am-3pm

The Carnation Valley is a wonderfully flat place to bicycle, with quiet
country roads and open farm lands. The Original Brown Bag Cafe and
Bakery is part of this scene, an old time cafe with great goodies for bicyclists.
Founded in 1979 by the current owner Alex Awasthi's father, it is located in a
building which was first erected in 1911. The bakery was created to provide
fresh breads and bakery products for the small cafe.

The signature product of the Original Brown Bag is their large, gooey
white-icing cinnamon rolls, but it is also well known for wonderful pies fresh-
baked by Thelma Bosma, a long time employee. In addition, you will find
pecan rolls, blueberry and cran-orange muffins, sticky buns, cornbread and
several types of bread. Thelma uses the fresh seasonal items grown in the
valley in many of her products. You can have a full breakfast or lunch, or
sample the delightful bakery products.

You will find indoor and outdoor seating (picnic tables with umbrellas)
and restrooms. If you want to buy a cinnamon roll and then go stretch out on
the grass, McDonald Park is just two blocks south. The owner welcomes
bicyclists and is a co-sponsor of Team Washington, a bicycle track racing
team that performs at Marymoor Velodrome.

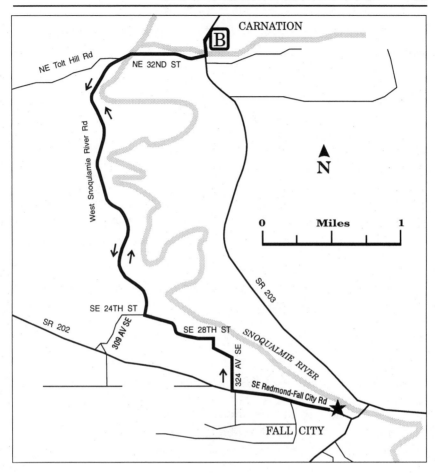

THE RIDE

This is a very easy ride that is flat and has little traffic. You will spend more time looking at cows than at cars. Relax on a back country road and enjoy the scenery.

Start: Fall City Memorial King County Park, Fall City. To get to Fall City, take I-90 east to the Preston exit 22. Turn left and take the first right onto Preston-Fall City Road SE and follow it to Fall City. Turn left at the stop sign in Fall City and park along the Fall City Memorial King County Park on the gravel.

Miles: 16.8

Difficulty: Easy. Flat.

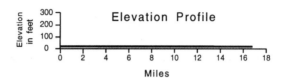

Mountain Bike variation: Go to Carnation on SR 203 and turn right (east) on Entwistle Street. Go four blocks to a small park on the right, Nick Loutsis Park. Take the trail to the right for 6.2 miles and return. For more information see Trip #8 in *Washington's Rail-Trails* by this author.

0.0   Start at Fall City Memorial King County Park, located between the Snoqualmie River and SE Redmond-Fall City Road across from the market in Fall City and head west on SR 202..

0.9   Right on 324th Ave. SE and wind along until road name changes several times and becomes SE 24th St. heading west.

2.6   Right on W Snoqualmie River Rd. SE.

6.8   Right on NE 32nd St. (NE Tolt Hill Rd.).

6.9   Cross Snoqualmie River on narrow bridge.

7.5   Left on Fall City-Carnation Rd. NE (SR 203).

7.5   Cross Tolt River on a narrow bridge.

8.2   Original Brown Bag Cafe and Bakery is on your right at the south end of town.

THE RETURN

8.2   Leave the Original Brown Bag Cafe and Bakery heading south, the way you came.

8.9   Cross Tolt River on narrow bridge.

8.9   Right on NE Tolt Hill Rd.

9.5   Left on W Snoqualmie River Rd. NE.

14.2   Left on SE 24th St., which eventually becomes 324th Ave. SE.

15.9   Left on SR 202 (SE Redmond-Fall City Rd.).

16.8   Fall City Memorial King County Park, Fall City.

RIDE 12

MEANDERING TO MONROE

The lower Snoqualmie Valley is a great place to bicycle. This ride
takes you between Duvall and Monroe via the West Snoqualmie
Valley Rd. and other backroads. You will pass many farms and
over a rickety old wood and metal bridge over the Snoqualmie
River with access to the water. It is a fairly flat, easy, out-and-back
ride with wonderful scenery.

SKY RIVER BAKERY

Owners: Karen Clifton, Mary Thorgerson and Andrew Abt
Address: 117 1/2 Main St., Monroe
Phone: 794-7434
Hours: Tues-Fri 7am-5pm; Sat 7am-4pm;
closed Sunday and Monday

Most of the businesses in Monroe have moved to the SR 2 highway strip
leaving main street a quiet place for bicyclists. Located near the bicycle route
through Monroe is a new bakery in an old location. It is a warm restful place
with bright colors, fresh flowers on the tables and a rotating display of
paintings, compliments of the Open Door Gallery just around the corner.

The Sky River Bakery came into existence when the three owners, tired
of working for others, created their own special place with high quality baked
products. Karen, Mary and Andrew have developed all the recipes, make
everything from scratch, do not fry anything and love their work. They enjoy
experimenting with new taste combinations and have produced more than fifty
varieties of scones.

Cookies include: snickerdoodle, chocolate chip, butterscotch cashew,
oatmeal raisin and sour cream chocolate. Muffins include: morning glory, sour
cream chocolate, blueberry, orange poppy seed, blackberry honey bran and
sugar-free. You can find pumpkin bars, butterhorns, cinnamon rolls, whole
wheat cinnamon rolls, rum pecan rolls, Italian sausage rolls, pecan sticky
buns, raspberry white chocolate coffeecake, apple almond danish, raspberry

cream cheese danish, mixed berry coffeecake, rosemary swiss cheese biscuit, biscotti -- well, you get the idea. Look for the use of "craisins" (dried cranberries) in many products.

The bakers also produce a variety of breads including: forgosa (parmesan, mozzarella, cheddar, swiss cheese, scallions, olive oil and parsley), chick-a-dee (sunflower, millet, poppyseed, seasame and flax seeds), five grain, Italian herb chedder, black pepper parmesan french baguettes, artichoke sun-dried tomato rustica, and sun-dried tomato and olive baguettes. They usually have pizza, quiche and make their own granola mix. One of the trademarks at Sky River Bakery is the use of fresh flowers on their custom cakes. For those people on your ride who are really acting like animals, you might offer them Gourmet Bowser Bones, although a real dog might enjoy them more.

To quench your thirst the Sky River Bakery offers espresso, Starbucks Coffee, Stash teas, seltzer, fruit juices and soft drinks including root beer. It also offers Deer Mountain Preserves made in Granite Falls, honey from Sunny Ridge Apiaries in Monroe and special greeting cards. You will find indoor seating, restrooms and wonderfully friendly service.

THE RIDE

This is a pleasant, flat ride through the Snoqualmie Valley, meandering past working farms, crossing the Snoqualmie and Skykomish Rivers and then following quiet back roads to Monroe.

Start: Duvall. Duvall is located on SR 203. **1) From I-90,** go east to the Preston exit 22 and turn left across freeway and then right on the Preston-Fall City Road. At Fall City go across the bridge and turn left on SR 203 north (Fall City-Carnation Rd. SE) through Carnation to Duvall. **2) From I-520,** go east to Redmond and then turn right on the Redmond-Fall City Road (SR 202) to Fall City then left on SR 203 north to Duvall. **3) From Bothell,** go east to Woodinville and take the Woodinville-Duvall Road. Park on the street or in the city park.

Miles: 21.5

Difficulty: Easy. Flat.

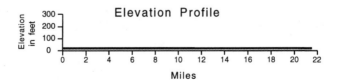

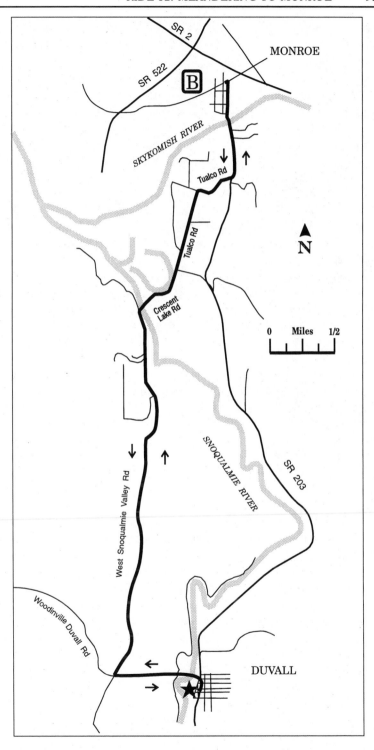

Kathy, Bill and Melissa at the Sky River Bakery.

0.0   Duvall. As point of reference, start at mini-mall at corner of Main St. (SR 203) and Stephens St. and head north.

0.2   Left on bridge over Snoqualmie River (NE Woodinville-Duvall Rd.)

1.4   Right on W Snoqualmie Valley Rd. NE (becomes High Bridge Rd.).

5.7   Right on Crescent Lake Rd.

7.0   Straight on Tualco Rd.

8.2   Continue right on Tualco Rd.

9.4   Left on SR 203.

10.2   Cross Skykomish River.

10.9   Left on Main St.

11.0   Sky River Bakery is on your right with a neon sign that proclaims "Bakery Open."

THE RETURN

11.0   Leave Sky River Bakery and return the way you came.

11.1   Right on Lewis St. which becomes SR 203.

11.8   Cross Skykomish River.

12.6   Right on Tualco Rd.

13.4   Continue left on Tualco Rd.

14.5   Continue straight on Tualco Rd.

14.7   Straight on Crescent Lake Rd.

15.9   Left on High Bridge Rd. (W Snoqualmie Valley Rd.).

20.2   Left on NE Woodinville-Duvall Rd.

21.4   Right on SR 203.

21.5   Duvall.

RIDE 13

A BIT OF WHIDBEY

When visiting the islands of Puget Sound, one floats away from the hubbub of the urban megalopolis. Here roads are less crowded, the countryside less developed. Whidbey has its share of hills, but this ride is not too steep nor too long. Langely is a very small, quaint town close to the ferry but bypassed by the main highway. It is an ideal short bicycle trip to an intimate place with a great view of Puget Sound and Camano Island and to a great new bakery.

LANGLEY VILLAGE BAKERY

Owner: Marie Bird-Legters
Address: 227 Second St., Langley
Phone: 221-3133
Hours: Mon-Sat 7:30am-5pm; Sun 8:30am-2:30pm

The Langley Village Bakery is a new bakery with the personal touch you'd expect to find in a small rural community. This is just like home-made. Marie Bird-Legters has been baking for the local Bayview Farmer's Market for years and, with the encouragement of friends, started this bakery so more people could share the treats.

The bakery is located in a small pedestrian-oriented shopping area on Second St. in Langley. It is a small, bright, triangle-shaped space with windows on two sides. The baked goods are simply and attractively displayed as befits their quality.

Marie is most famous for her Country Italian bread which takes a long time to make -- three days from start to finish. Another specialty is the fricosse which is a round French bread filled with pesto, cheese and tomatoes and comes in both a small and large size. A third specialty is the pain de seigle (French sour rye), a bread with a hard crust that lasts for days (if you don't eat it first).

There is an assortment of other baked products including croissants, large fruit danish, bread pudding with vanilla sauce, large white and whole wheat cinnamon rolls, apple strudel, muffins and cookies including wimpy's jumbles (a large mound of chocolate chips, hazelnuts, pecans and raisins).

Marie Bird-Legters displays her wonderful breads.

You will find Caffe Mauro espresso and coffee, tea, soft drinks, two small indoor tables, an outside south facing courtyard and very warm, friendly service.

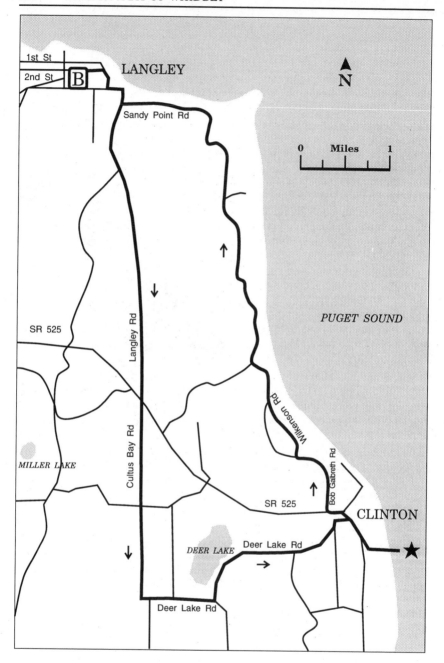

THE RIDE

This is a scenic ride to the picturesque little town of Langley on Whidbey Island. There are a number of hills along the route although none are very strenuous. The climb from the ferry dock is probably the biggest challenge. When in Langley, be sure to explore the other small shops and the view north from First St.

Start: Mukilteo State Park Boat Launch, Mukilteo. From I-5, take the Mukilteo exit 182 to downtown Mukilteo. **Please take note of the current parking restrictions.** These rules are so that there will be parking for boaters early in the mornings.

Miles: 15.4

Difficulty: Moderate. Some hills.

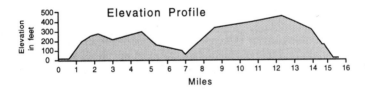

0.0   Start at the Mukilteo State Park Boat Launch.

0.2   Turn right on Mukilteo Speedway and go up hill to toll booths, buy a ticket and descend down to ferry dock on the left side in front of the waiting room.

0.4   Board ferry. (See introduction about ferries.)

0.6   Exit ferry and begin climb of a long, steep hill. You might want to wait until the ferry traffic unloads.

1.3   Right on Bob Galbreth Rd.

2.2   Right on Wilkenson Rd.

3.0   Continue right on Wilkenson Rd.

5.4   Left on Sandy Point Rd.

6.2   Right at the unsigned T intersection.

6.8   Right at the stop sign (First St.).

6.9   Left on Second St.

7.0   Langley Village Bakery is on your left.

THE RETURN

7.0   Leave the Langley Village Bakery and head east out Second St.,
       returning the way you came.

7.1   Right on First St.

7.2   Left at stop sign.

7.5   Continue right on Langley Rd.

10.7   Cross SR 525. You are now on Cultus Bay Rd.

12.3   Left on Deer Lake Rd.

13.0   Continue left on Deer Lake Rd.

14.5   Right on Deer Lake St., then right on SR 525 heading downhill to ferry.

15.1   Board ferry and rest after a great ride.

15.2   Exit the ferry. Turn right and then left into the Mukilteo State Park
       Boat Launch.

15.4   Mukilteo State Park Boat Launch.

RIDE 14

THE CARNA-VALL RIDE

This loop ride connects *Carna*tion and Du*vall*. You will climb through the back woods east of Duvall and drop down back into the valley just before Carnation. After stopping at the Original Brown Bag Cafe and Bakery in Carnation (See Ride 11), you will pass by the world famous Carnation Dairy Farms (hold your nose). It is generally quite an easy ride, but there is some elevation gain.

Start: Duvall. Duvall is located on SR 203. **1) From I-90**, go east to the Preston exit 22 and turn left across the freeway and then right on the Preston-Fall City Road. At Fall City go across the bridge and turn left on SR 203 north. **2) From I-520**, go east to Redmond and then turn right on the Redmond-Fall City Road to Fall City. **3) From Bothell**, go east to Woodinville and take the Woodinville-Duvall Road. Park on the street, in the city park under the bridge or in the park just south of town on SR 203.

Miles: 24.5

Difficulty: Moderate. One long grade.

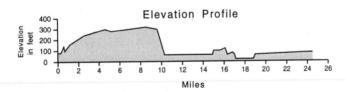

0.0 Leave Duvall and head **north** on SR 203. (As point of reference, start at mini-mall at corner of Main St. (SR 203) and Stephens St.)

0.3 Right on NE Cherry Valley Rd. There is a steep climb for a little way, so gear down.

4.6 Continue right and straight on Kelly Rd. through several intersections.

9.6 Begin steep descent with a "T" intersection at bottom.

10.3 Left on SR 203.

13.2 Original Brown Bag Cafe and Bakery.

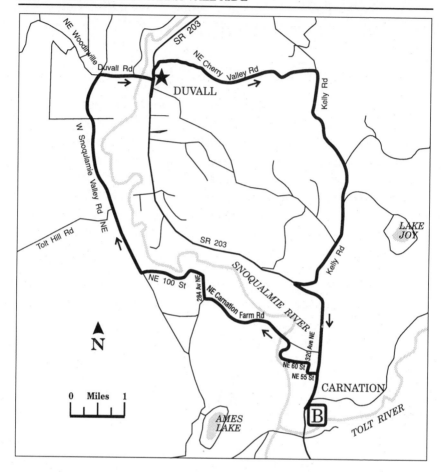

THE RETURN

13.2   Start at the Original Brown Bag Cafe and Bakery in Carnation and head north on SR 203.

13.6   Left on NE 55th St. This is a very small city street and can easily be missed. (If you do miss it, turn left at NE 60th St.)

13.7   Right on 320th Ave. NE.

14.0   Left on NE 60th St.

15.0   Hard left onto NE Carnation Farm Rd. and cross Snoqualmie River.

17.0   Right on 284th Ave. NE. CAUTION! Not passable at high water.

17.5   Continue left on NE 100th St.

19.0   Right on W Snoqualmie Valley Rd. NE.

20.5   Straight on W Snoqualmie Valley Rd. NE.

23.4   Right on NE Woodinville-Duvall Rd.

24.5   Right on Carnation-Duvall Rd. (SR 203 or Main St.) in Duvall.

RIDE 15

HIGH BRIDGE ROAD

This is a wonderful country road ride between two great country bakeries, the Sky River Bakery and the Sweet Life Cafe. This is the ride that local bicyclists take visitors on when they want to show off the great cycling opportunities in this region. It has everything you could want: quiet back roads, good views, manageable hills and great food stops. (For information on the Sky River Bakery, see Ride 12.)

THE SWEET LIFE CAFE

Owners: Paula Inman and Dennis Lebow
Address: 1024 1st St. #201, Snohomish
Phone: 568-3554
Hours: Tues-Sat 9am-9pm; Sun 9am-5pm

Paula Inman and Dennis LeBow have indeed created the Sweet Life for their customers. Located upstairs on the mezzanine level of the old Marks Building in historic Snohomish, the Sweet Life is a small, intimate cafe with great food and bakery products. Having worked at a fancy, downtown Seattle restaurant, the owners know good food but prefer the relaxed atmosphere of a small town.

Having just ridden from Monroe, you have earned the right to try a cream cheese brownie, date bar, lemon bar, apple streusel bar, pear crisp, bread pudding, or a slice of chocolate bundt cake, carrot cake or coffee cake. The Sweet Life also serves muffins, scones, croissants and bagels. If you are feeling really proud of your riding effort, try the "ultimate decadence" (yes, it's all chocolate).

This is a full service restaurant with wine and beer. Some of the tables are located next to the front windows where you have a great view down on the activities on 1st St. Park your bicycles at the bike rack on the west side of the building or across the street where you can keep an eye on them.

At the Sweet Life you will find a warm cozy atmosphere, high quality food, espresso and restrooms. After you eat and before you head out of town again, be sure to stroll around for a while. The old part of Snohomish is an historical area and has numerous antique and other speciality shops.

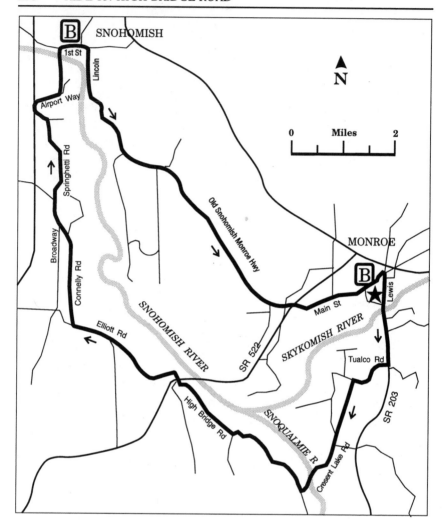

THE RIDE

Start: Sky River Bakery, Monroe. From I-5, go east on I-520, north on I-405 and take the Monroe exit 23 onto SR 522. Turn off SR 522 at the Main St. exit and head east. Follow Main St. to just before the light in downtown Monroe. The bakery is on your left. You can park on the street in the block west of the bakery or turn right on Lewis St. and go south 0.4 miles to the park on your left.

Miles: 24.4

Difficulty: Moderate. Some hills

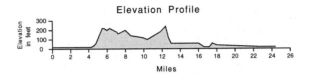

0.0 Leave Sky River Bakery heading east.

0.1 Right on Lewis St.

0.7 Cross Skykomish River.

1.6 Right on Tualco Rd.

2.3 Continue left on Tualco Rd.

3.6 Continue straight on Crescent Lake Rd.

4.4 Climb up wooden bridge that is narrow and fairly long with poor sight distance behind you. CAUTION! Do not stop on the bridge to admire the water below or you may end up in it!

4.6 Right on High Bridge Rd.

5.5 Cross over the "high bridge" named because of the distance to the bottom of the creek below. This was a wooden structure until 1991.

6.0 View northeast on right.

6.6 Continue right on High Bridge Rd.

6.7 Pass Old Cider Mill on right which serves fresh cider in season.

7.1 Great view east up the Skykomish River. The confluence of the Skykomish and Snoqualmie Rivers is just below you. The combined rivers become the Snohomish River.

7.2 Stop sign. Cross narrow wooden bridge.

8.6 Pass under SR 522. Road becomes Elliott Rd.

10.4 Right on Connelly Rd.

11.8 Pass under railroad tracks. Watch for oncoming traffic.

12.4 Right on Broadway and begin steep descent.

12.7 Right on Springhetti Rd. There are two yellow farm tractor signs at the entrance to Springhetti.

14.7 Straight on Airport Way.

15.6 CAUTION! Cross rough railroad tracks.

15.9 Right on 1st St.

16.0 Sweet Life Bakery is on your left.

THE RETURN

16.0   Leave the Sweet Life behind heading east (uphill on 1st St.) and keep right at the "Y" at the top of the hill.

16.2   Cross railroad tracks with caution.

16.5   Right on Lincoln which becomes Old Snohomish-Monroe Highway.

16.8   Pass under railroad tracks. CAUTION! This is a very narrow passageway.

16.9   Cross rough narrow bridge.

22.6   Pass under SR 522.

22.7   Enter Monroe city limits.

24.3   Very tall flag pole. If the flag is pointing away from you, then you are not as strong as you thought and you need to stop at the bakery. If it is pointing towards you, you have earned the right to stop at the bakery.

24.4   Sky River Bakery on left.

Enjoying the backroads of Snohomish County.

RIDE 16

SNOQUALMIE RIVER TOUR

This ride takes you over the three main forks of the Snoqualmie River, over the main channel of the Snoqualmie River and past the famous Snoqualmie Falls. You will have to climb one long hill to get to what is called the upper Snoqualmie River Valley, but the views are worth the climb. Pause in North Bend at George's Bakery and then coast back down to Fall City.

GEORGE'S BAKERY

Owner:	Greg and Cornelia Cordova
Address:	127 North Bend Way, North Bend
Phone:	888-0632
Hours:	Tues-Fri 6:30am-6:00pm; Sat 7:30am-6pm; Sun 8:30am-5pm; **closed Monday**

In the heart of North Bend is located a bakery which symbolizes the slowly increasing change that has occurred in this area. The bakery was originally opened in 1921 by Mr. Ballinger who served the community until 1964. George Macris took over from Ballinger and became a fixture in North Bend for the next 29 years. Now it is Greg and Cornelia Cordova's turn. They took over in 1993 and are bringing to George's the types of changes occurring throughout the North Bend area. They have added espresso, whole wheat products and a much wider variety. However, they have retained some of the history of the place including the famous crushed wheat bread.

The crushed wheat bread is baked from a sixty year old recipe. It is made with honey, brown sugar and white flour, and baked in cylindrical pans. It is an unusual and popular bread with a light and delicate taste. Greg and Cornelia make a number of breads on different days in addition to the crushed wheat, including cinnamon wheat, an attractive dark, braided loaf.

Looking for calories? Try rocky road cookies (marshmallow, walnuts, chocolate), rum balls, rum-filled florentines, coconut bon-bons, granola bars, 9-grain energy bars, walnut shortbread, english toffee cookies, caramel honey walnut squares, fruit tarts or pies. There are mazurkas, some sugarless cookies, bagels, muffins, numerous coffee cakes, danish, apple fritters, bear claws, cookies and peanut butter shortbread.

In addition to the sweets, you will find fresh salads, pizza by the slice, quiche, soups, espresso, coffee, Stash tea and soft drinks. There is inside seating, bathrooms and a park around the corner behind the old railroad station, where you can take your pastries on beautiful days.

THE RIDE

This ride is very scenic with one big uphill. It passes close to Snoqualmie Falls overlook which you can stop to enjoy, has a splendid view up and down the valley from above the Weyerhauser Mill site and travels alongside various forks and sections of the Snoqualmie River.

Start: Fall City Memorial King County Park, Fall City. To get to Fall City, take I-90 east to the Preston exit 22. Turn left and take the first right onto Preston-Fall City Road and follow it to Fall City. Turn left at the stop sign in Fall City and park along the Fall City Memorial King County Park on the gravel.

Miles: 22.3

Difficulty: Moderate. One long hill.

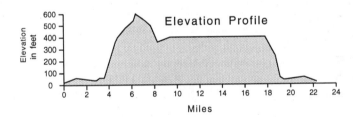

0.0   Start at Fall City Memorial King County Park, located between the Snoqualmie River and the Redmond-Fall City Road, across from the market in Fall City. Head east on SR 202.

0.2   Left over bridge on SR 202 and continue right (east).

1.1   Right on SE Fish Hatchery Rd.

2.9   Left on 372nd Ave. SE.

3.2   Right on SR 202. Tokul Creek Fish Hatchery is on your right with restrooms.

3.6   Cross Tokul Creek, begin long climb.

4.6   Snoqualmie Falls overlook on your right. Restrooms, view of falls.

4.8   Pass under pedestrian walkway at crest of hill, turn left on Tokul Rd.

5.5   Pass over Snoqualmie Valley Rail-Trail.

6.2   Keep right on 396th Ave. SE.

6.5   Continue on 396th Ave. SE.

8.3   Left on SE Reinig Rd. along Snoqualmie River.

10.1   Right on 428th Ave. SE.

10.2   Cross North Fork Snoqualmie River.

10.6   Optional: You can detour left at the dead end sign and cross an old bridge which is an historic landmark noted for its age and type of construction.

11.4   Continue right on NE 12th St. (SE 108th St.).

12.1   Continue left on 420th Ave. SE.

12.4   Continue right on Ballarat Ave. N.

12.7   Right on North Bend Way.

12.8   George's Bakery on your left (south side of street).

THE RETURN

12.8   Leave George's Bakery heading west (left).

12.8   Right on North Bend Blvd. at the light.

13.0   Continue left on SR 202.

13.2   CAUTION! Cross a very narrow, busy bridge over the South Fork Snoqualmie River. Use extreme caution!

13.6   Right on Boalch Ave. NW which immediately turns into Meadowbrook-North Bend Rd SE.

15.3   Right on Park St.

15.7   Cross Snoqualmie River on a narrow, rough bridge and take a hard left on unmarked flat road (Mill Pond Rd).

16.4   The lumber mill pond is on your right.

17.2   Continue left on Mill Pond Rd (unmarked).

17.3   Right on SR 202.

17.6   Snoqualmie Falls overlook is on your left.

19.1   Left on 372nd Ave. SE.

19.4   Right on SE Fish Hatchery Rd.

21.2   Left on SR 202.

22.0   Left over bridge and right on SR 202.

22.3   Fall City Memorial King County Park in Fall City.

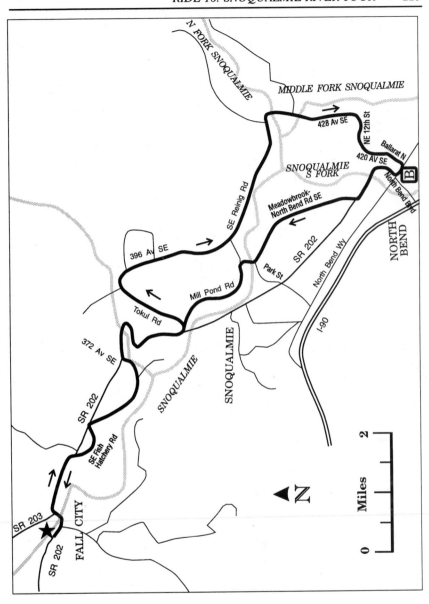

RIDE 17

SIDE ROADS TO SULTAN

Sultan is east of Monroe on the very busy SR 2, the road to Stevens Pass. This ride shows you a way to make a loop ride from Monroe to Sultan and return staying mostly off of SR 2. You will find great views and quiet side roads. There are two very short steep hills, both of which can be walked if necessary.

SULTAN BAKERY

Owners: Daryle and Carol Jacobson
Address: 711 Stevens Pass Highway, Sultan
Phone: 793-2434
Hours: Mon-Thurs 6am-5pm; Fri-Sun 6am-7pm

The Sultan Bakery has more than enough calories to satisfy the hungriest bicyclist. Portions are large and sweet. For the ultimate energy boost, try their **one pound brownies** made of two layers with fudge in between. You will either be full of energy or sick.

The bakery items include a wide selection of doughnuts, danish, apple fritters and fruit strudels. Thanks to the Jacobsons' Swedish background, they provide many Swedish items including Swedish brownies (dipped in chocolate), breads and lefse (a flat bread made with potatoes and flour). There are fancy cakes, pies, cookies and many breads.

Additional edibles include: Vivian's Ice Cream on the Sultan Bakery's own fresh-made cones, sandwiches made from their fresh bread, many deli items and a soup de jour. You will find soft drinks, espresso, restrooms, inside seating and outside picnic tables.

THE RIDE

This is a backroads ride that takes you up to broad views and along the Skykomish River. There are some very steep and short climbs, but the roads are generally free of traffic, except for brief sections of SR 2.

Start: Sky River Bakery, Monroe (see Ride 12). From I-5, go east on I-520, north on I-405, and take the Monroe exit 23 onto SR 522. Turn off

SR 522 at the Main St. exit and head east. Follow Main St. to just before the light in downtown Monroe. The bakery is on your left. You can park on the street in the block west of the bakery or turn right on Lewis St. and go south 0.4 miles to the park on your left.

Miles: 22.7

Difficulty: Moderate. Two steep uphills.

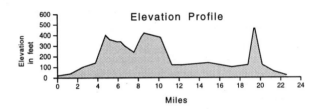

Shortcut: An easier alternative from Monroe is to go straight at milepost 0.1 across SR 2 and take Old Owen Rd. This saves about 4 miles and avoids climbing a steep, short hill. Reconnect with the ride at mile 10.2.

0.0   Leave the Sky River Bakery in Monroe and head east.

0.1   Left on Stevens Pass Highway (SR 2) and immediately turn right onto Woods Creek Rd. CAUTION! There is a lot of traffic at this intersection.

2.0   Right on Yeagar Rd.

3.8   Right on Bollenbaugh Hill Rd. Prepare for a short but very steep hill climb of 0.2 mile.

4.8   Right on 120th St. SE (Florence Acres Loop) and immediately right on 247th Ave. SE.

5.4   Continue left on 124th St. SE.

5.9   Continue right on 251st Ave. SE.

6.2   Left on 132nd St. SE.

6.4   Right on 259th Ave. SE.

6.7   Left on Florence Acres Rd.

7.5   Continue left briefly on 271st Ave. SE and then continue right on Florence Acres Rd.

8.6   Right on Woods Lake Rd.

10.2   Left on Old Owen Rd.

10.7   Start of very steep descent.

11.3   Left on SR 2. CAUTION! Cross this road carefully and note that the bridge ahead is very narrow with no shoulder.

12.3   Sultan Bakery is on your left with a large "Bakery" sign.

THE RETURN

12.3   Leave Sultan Bakery and head west (right) on SR 2.

12.4   Left on 311th Ave. SE (Mann Rd.). This is the road that goes over the railroad tracks and then a small bridge.

13.3   Right on Ben Howard Rd.

18.8   Bottom of a very steep but short hill. It is a little longer than your first climb on Bollenbaugh Hill Rd.

19.4   Top of hill, very steep descent.

21.6   Right on SR 203.

21.8   Cross bridge over Skykomish River.

22.0   Pass Al Borlen Park on right with restrooms, grass.

22.6   Left on Main St.

22.7   Sky River Bakery on your right.

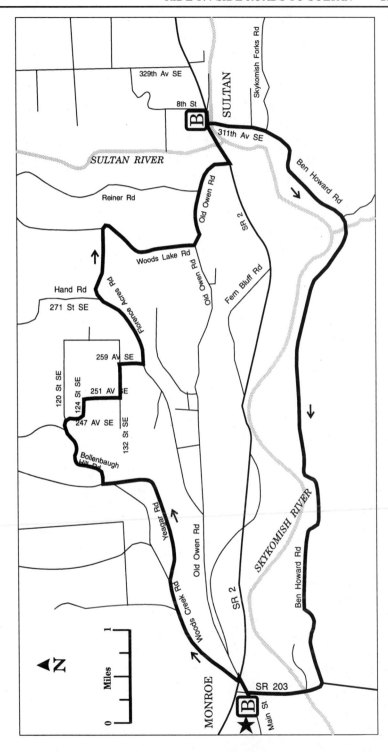

RIDE 18

TULIP TOWN TOUR

The Skagit Flats are home to many tulip farms and in the early spring the land becomes a blanket of bright colors from flowers in bloom. This ride will show you a great route between Mt. Vernon and LaConner. Try not to do this ride on a windy day because the flatness will be less apparent when you're fighting stiff head winds. Mt. Vernon is a thriving old town, LaConner an exploding tourist town. Between both you will find solace in flat roads and great views in all directions.

THE CALICO CUPBOARD

Owner:	Linda Freed
Address:	720 S 1st St., LaConner
Phone:	466-4451
Hours:	Mon-Fri 7:30am-5pm; Sat-Sun 7:30am-5:30pm

LaConner used to be a small fishing community near the mouth of the Skagit River. Today it is a popular tourist town with many little shops to explore. One place worth stopping is the Calico Cupboard, a restaurant with great baked goods.

The Calico Cupboard was started by Linda Freed as a place serving high quality food. She has created a very attractive little cafe with award winning recipes. It is a great place to pick up some wholesome bakery products or to get a complete meal.

Bicyclists will love the selection of baked goods. For those with a yearning for sweets, try the Hilary bars (peanut and oatmeal), fudgy-wudgy brownies (walnut brownie with cream cheese) or Rocky Road bars (brownie, cream cheese, marshmallow and fudge topping). They have whole wheat cinnamon rolls, caramel sticky buns, lemon poppyseed scones, large cookies (ginger molasses, oatmeal raisin, snickerdoodle, peanut chocolate chunk), morning glory muffins, croissants (plain, almond, raspberry, apple, ham and cheese), large gooey apple dumplings, caramel nut rolls, very large almond macaroons, bread-pudding, berry coffeecake and "blu-barb crunch." Breads include: French and multi-grain baguettes, cornmeal molasses, onion dill, honey wheat and Country Fair Egg. A special treat is the "Fugassa" bread with tomatoes, green peppers, onions, olives and chedder cheese.

To satisfy your thirst as well as your hunger, the Calico Cupboard offers coffee, espresso, beer and wine, Italian sodas, iced lattes and espresso ice cream melt-a-way's. Not only does the restaurant offer full breakfast and lunch menus, there are also special children's menus equipped with crayons. You will also find restrooms, a small porch out back and a riverside park just around the west corner of the building.

THE RIDE

This is an easy, scenic ride across the Skagit flats; however, if it is a windy day you will have a real workout. A particularly beautiful month of the year for this ride is April, during the annual Skagit Valley Tulip Festival. The fields you pass will be filled with colorful tulips and, if travelling by bicycle, will give you an olfactory and visual treat. Go early and avoid the car traffic.

Start: City Bakery, Mt. Vernon (see Ride 27). From I-5 take the Mt. Vernon exit 226. Turn left (west) and continue straight across railroad tracks. Turn right on S 1st St. You can park in the public parking lots to the west of the 1st St. storefronts.

Miles: 30.7

Difficulty: Moderate. Flat.

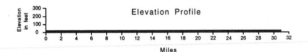

0.0   Leave City Bakery, Mt. Vernon, and head north on S 1st St.
0.2   Left on W Division St. and cross bridge over Skagit River.
0.4   Left on Baker St., beyond Schwinn Bicycle store.
0.6   Right on Ball St. (Behrns-Millett Rd.).
1.8   Continue left on Penn Rd.
2.8   Right on Calhoun Rd.
6.5   Left on Best Rd.
6.9   Right on Rudene Rd. (this is a short cut-off to Chilberg Rd.).
7.0   Right on Chilberg Rd.

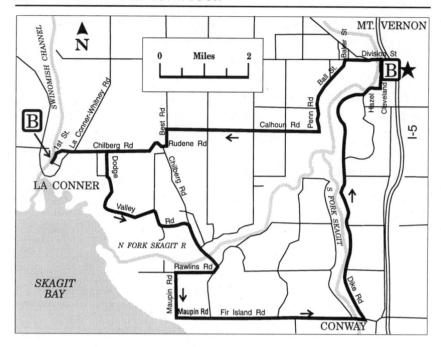

9.1   Straight on LaConner-Whitney Rd. and continue straight to downtown on Morris St.

9.5   Left on S 1st St.

9.7   The Calico Cupboard is at the end of the block on the right.

THE RETURN

9.7   Leave the Calico Cupboard and head east (left).

9.9   Turn right on Morris St.

10.3   Continue straight through intersection on Chilberg Rd.

11.5   Right on Dodge Valley Rd.

14.1   Right on Chilberg Rd.

16.1   Right on Rawlins Rd. before fruit stand.

16.8   Left on Maupin Rd.

18.6   Straight on Fir Island Rd.

22.2   The small community of Conway is on your right.

22.5   Left on Dike Rd., just over the South Fork Skagit River.

29.2   Left on Hazel St.

30.2   Left on Cleveland.

30.7   City Bakery, Mt. Vernon, is on your right.

RIDE 19

STILLY FOOTHILLS RAMBLE

"Stilly" is the locals' name for the Stillaguamish River which passes through Granite Falls and Arlington. The river cuts a deep, spectacular gorge through the terrain, which is, unfortunately, usually invisible from the roads. This route provides several glimpses and approaches to the river, including an optional shortcut over a suspension bridge (see note below) that gives views up and down the Stilly.

COUNTRY BAKERY

Owner: Dennis Jarman
Address: 324 Olympic Ave., Arlington
Phone: 453-2866
Hours: Tues-Sat 6:30am-5pm;
closed Sunday and Monday

Nestled along the main street in downtown Arlington is the suitably named "Country Bakery." Arlington is still a country town, although that is slowly changing as the population pressures are creeping north from Seattle.

This small town bakery is unpretentious in its appearance. It proudly displays its baked goods in the sidewalk bay window, acting as an enticement to all those who pass by. There are ample seats indoors for the frequent regular customers and visitors alike. You won't find any espresso, but Dennis does provide ample coffee.

The owner Dennis Jarman has been a baker for 39 years. He does all the baking himself and also seems to know most of his customers. You will find traditional American-style pastries such as apple fritters, cinnamon rolls, blueberry popovers, cookies, muffins, and for the hungry cyclist, huge Texas sized doughnuts.

THE RIDE

Start: Granite Falls. From I-5, take the Snohomish exit 194 turning right (east) on SR 2. Turn left on SR 204, left on SR 9 and right on SR 92 to Granite Falls. Turn right at the only light in town onto Granite Ave. Park in the Park and Ride lot on your left, about two blocks down. It is a gravel lot behind the small bus shelter.

Miles: 27.6

Difficulty: Moderate. Some hills, some narrow roads.

Shortcut: At mile 6.7 take the Jordon Bridge (suspension bridge mentioned above) across the Stillaguamish River, climb steeply up Jordan Trails Rd. and regain the route at milepost 24.1. This shortens the ride to only 10 miles, but the climb up Jordan Trails Rd. is quite steep.

0.0   Leave Park and Ride in Granite Falls and head north on Granite Ave.
0.3   Left at light on SR 92.
0.6   Right on Jordan Rd. just past large SR 92 sign.
1.8   Cross Stillaguamish River.
6.7   Jordan. The Jordan Bridge, a rebuilt suspension bridge, is on your left across from the old Jordan store.
7.7   Terrace Falls is across the river to your left. In the spring, after a heavy rain, this is a large waterfall.
9.8   River Meadows Park, Snohomish Parks. This park along the river has a steep gravel road and a large grassy area at the bottom.
12.7   Left on Arlington Heights Rd.
13.7   Left on SR 530.
14.1   Cross narrow bridge going uphill.
14.3   Continue right on Burke Ave.
14.5   Left on Broadway.
14.6   Right on Division St. Immediately get in far left lane.
14.7   Left on Olympic Ave.
14.9   Country Bakery is under the "Bakery" sign at 324 Olympic Ave.

THE RETURN

14.9   Leave the Country Bakery and head south on Olympic Ave.
15.0   Left on 3rd St.
15.1   Right on French Ave.
15.6   Left on Highland Dr.
15.8   Right on Stillaguamish Ave. (83rd Ave. NE).

16.0   Bottom of hill on Burn Rd. This is a long, steep hill.

18.3   Top of steep part of Burn Rd.

20.5   Pass Jordan Trails Rd. Jordan Bridge over Stillaguamish River is down this road.

24.1   Left (straight) on 116th St. NE (W Engebretsen Rd.).

24.6   Stillaguamish River is on your left.

26.5   Right on Jordan Rd. (187th Ave. NE).

27.0   Left on SR 92.

27.3   Right on Granite Ave.

27.6   Granite Falls Park and Ride.

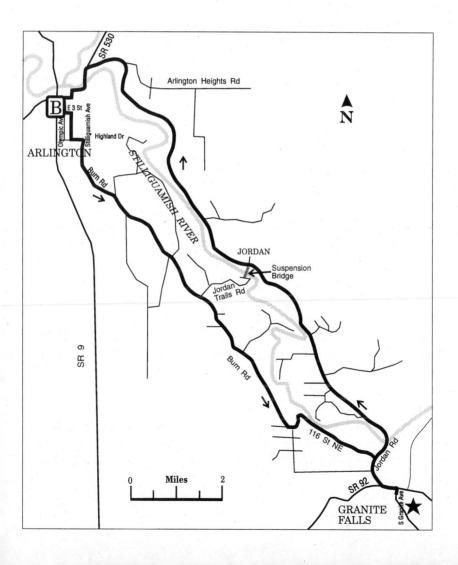

RIDE 20

VASHON VANQUISHED

After you have climbed the hill from the ferry you will have a better understanding of the name for this ride. Vashon Island is a very hilly place. But it is also a very lovely country place, isolated from the mainland with only ferries connecting it. Here you will take a short tour and find the country friendliness and high quality of baking produced at Bob's Bakery. Before or after you ride, stop in the Original Bakery near the Fauntleroy ferry terminal and enjoy the neighborhood feel of the Original Bakery.

THE ORIGINAL BAKERY

Owner:	Bernie Alonzo
Address:	9253 45th Ave. SW, Fauntleroy
Phone:	938-5088
Hours:	Tues-Fri 7:30am-6pm; Sat 7:30am-5pm;
	Sun 8am-4pm; **closed Monday**

The Original Bakery is a neighborhood bakery with the favorite traditional baked goods. It has not changed significantly since it was first opened in 1940 by Bill Latta. It was then sold to Mr. Dunbar who retired as a baker after fifty years of service. Bernie Alonzo took over in 1975.

Not only do Bernie's pastries taste great, he also works hard to make them very attractive, with special touches like the butterfly shapes of his danish. The selection includes: various doughnuts, raspberry bear claws, beautiful butterfly danish, almond danish, sliced bundt cakes, scones, sugar cookies, cinnamon rolls, apple fritters and cookies. A speciality is Seven Sisters Coffee Cake with several types of fruit fillings combined in one cake. There are also croissants, brioche, several types of breads, small pizzas and several whole wheat items.

You will find espresso, coffee, inside seating and greeting cards. It is a great place to wait for the next ferry to arrive before you start this ride, or a great place to finish off the day and pick up some goodies to take home.

Bernie Alonzo, owner and head baker at The Original Bakery.

BOB'S BAKERY

Owner: Bob Long
Address: 17506 Vashon Highway SW, Vashon Center,
Vashon Island
Phone: 463-5666
Hours: Tues-Fri 7am-6pm; Sat 9am-5pm;
closed Sunday and Monday

Welcome to a small, intimate, yet lively bakery. Here you will find flowers on the walls, in the windows and on the counter. You will also find delicious pastries and baked goods and super friendly service. Warning! This bakery is very popular. Get here early on Saturday morning or there won't be anything left. In fact, Bob usually has the front door open at 4:00 AM for the locals to come browsing through.

Bob Long is a friendly baker who constantly banters back and forth with his co-workers and with the steady stream of customers who wander back into the cooking area. Bob has been baking for 35 years and obviously loves his profession. All products are made with butter, not oil, and they use organic stone-ground flour. All products are made by hand.

If you want some calories, try the chocolate cream cheese brownies. The maple bars are special in that they are not deep fried and they have both a light body and excellent taste. The light frosting compliments rather than covers up the taste of the bar.

In addition to rich pastries, there are a variety of croissants, spinach rolls and quiche. For a nutritious meal, try Bob's Burger -- a whole wheat croissant, two kinds of olives and cheese, topped with pumpkin seeds. This was created by Bob for something to eat for his "lunch", and he continues to eat one almost every day.

You will find Guatemalan thick coffee but no espresso (try Seattle's Best Coffee, 2 miles south), restrooms, a park across the street (location of the Saturday market), great people and great food. Bicyclists will feel especially at home since the building was once a bike shop and Bob is an avid bicyclist in addition to being a great baker.

THE RIDE

This wonderful ride has a number of hills, the most significant of which occurs when you first get off the ferry. The hills are part of the character of Vashon Island and they are worth climbing just to get to Bob's Bakery. Before or after the ride, stop in at the Original Bakery. It is just south of the

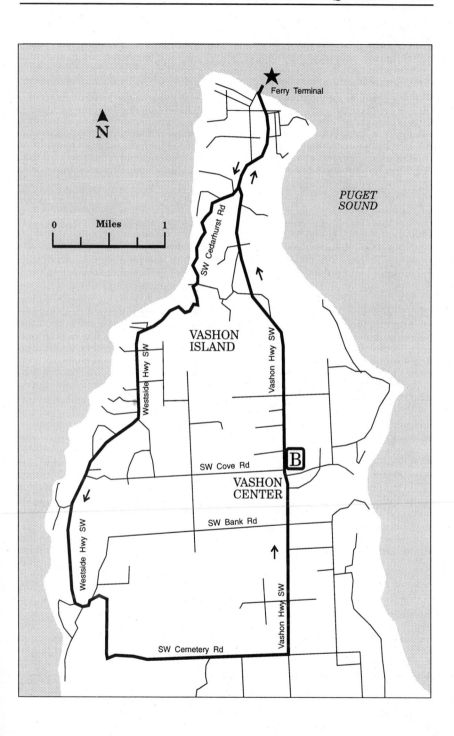

Fauntleroy Dock and to the left on Wildwood Place in the Fauntleroy
Shopping Mall at Wildwood Place and 45th Ave. SW.

Start: Lincoln Park, West Seattle. From I-5, take the Spokane
Street exit 163. Stay on Fauntleroy Way and turn left on Fauntleroy Ave. SW
which takes you directly to Lincoln Park. There is a parking lot at the south
end of Lincoln Park for day use only.

Miles: 16.9

Difficulty: Difficult. Steep hills.

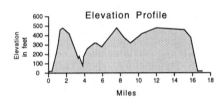

0.0   Lincoln Park. Leave and turn right on Fauntleroy Way.
0.1   Right onto Fauntleroy Dock. Take the ferry to Vashon.
0.3   Begin climb up long, steep hill on Vashon Highway SW.
2.3   Right on SW Cedarhurst Rd. (Corbin Rd. SW).
4.3   Continue right on SW Cedarhurst Rd.
5.3   Continue right on Westside Highway SW.
8.4   Left on SW Cemetery Rd.
9.3   Vashon Cemetery on right at top of hill.
9.7   The Bike Shop is on your left up a dirt road located in a barn and it's
       usually open weekends.
10.4   Left on Vashon Highway SW. Seattle's Best Coffee, 25 cents!
12.0   Bob's Bakery is just past the main light in Vashon Center on the right
       hand side of Vashon Highway SW.

THE RETURN

12.0   Leave Bob's Bakery heading the same direction you were traveling,
       north. Stay on Vashon Highway SW to the ferry dock.
15.7   Top of the same long, steep hill you climbed at the beginning of the day.
       Enjoy the ride down, but watch for cars parked on right shoulder
       waiting for the ferry. Use the traffic lane and go to the front of the line.
16.6   Vashon Heights Dock. Take ferry to Fauntleroy.
16.8   Exit the ferry and turn left on Fauntleroy Ave. SW. (Don't forget to
       stop at The Original Bakery if you didn't do so earlier.)
16.9   Left into parking for Lincoln Park.

RIDE 21

DON'T BE LEFSE BEHIND

Wander across the flat farmland of the lower Stillaguamish to find out what this name really means. Find out what makes those Scandinavians so strong. Stoke up on an assortment of baked goods at the Scandia Bakery in Stanwood so you won't be left behind and then wander back through the farms and woods to Arlington.

SCANDIA BAKERY AND LEFSE FACTORY

Owners: Don Haugon and Ken Turner
Address: 8706 271st St. NW, Stanwood
Phone: 629-2411
Hours: Tues-Sat 8am-5pm; **closed Sunday and Monday**

This is a large, friendly bakery that features lefsa, plenty of sweet bakery products and continuous polka music. What is lefsa? It is a traditional flat bread made of mashed potatoes and flour. This bakery is famous because it is still the only lefse factory west of the Mississippi River. The lefse formula and grills came from Holly, Minnesota, back in 1971 and were brought here by Don Haugon to provide some traditional flavor to the large Scandinavian community that lives in the Stanwood area.

Scandia Bakery specialties include: lefse, Swedish rye bread, coffee cake, Pritikin bread, fruit cake without citron and mocha florentines. You will also find all kinds of danish pastries, cookies, eclairs, turnovers, muffins and a full range of breads.

In addition to baked goods the bakery serves sandwiches, soups, espresso and coffee. There is plenty of inside seating, restrooms and an inside entrance to the Snow Goose Bookstore next door.

THE RIDE

This is a delightful country ride that shows off the beautiful rural country of the lower Stillaguamish. You will ride over the Stillaguamish, beside it and through farm land along the entire route.

Start: Country Bakery, Arlington. From I-5 take the northern Arlington exit 208. Follow SR 530 into Arlington and turn right on Olympic

Ave. Park on the street or one block east on the street. You can also park at
Haller Park located 0.3 miles north on SR 9, just before the bridge.

Miles: 33.8

Difficulty: Moderate. A few steep hills.

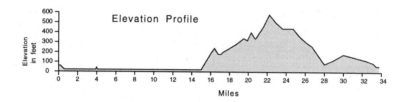

0.0   Start at the Country Bakery in Arlington. Go north on Olympic Ave.
0.2   Turn left on Division St. (which becomes SR 530) and continue
       straight.
4.0   Cross over I-5.
6.6   Enter Silvana. Faye's Country Cafe, grocery, Viking Hall.
7.5   Cross Stillaguamish River. Stop by the Little White Church on the Hill
       just out of town after you cross the river. Examine the names on the
       tombstones to get a feel for the age of the Scandinavian community in
       this area.
7.7   Left on Norman Rd.
9.9   Stillaguamish River on left.
12.1   Continue straight on Norman Rd. over bridge.
12.6   Right on Marine Dr.
14.7   Continue straight on Florence Rd. Re-cross Stillaguamish River and
       continue into downtown Stanwood.
14.9   Left on 271st St. NW.
15.0   Scandia Bakery on left with wood shingled store front.

THE RETURN

15.0   Leave Scandia Bakery and head straight east.
15.1   CAUTION! Four sets of bad railroad tracks. Cross with care.
15.2   Continue straight up center road through tunnel under highway.
15.6   Continue straight and keep left onto 80th Ave. NW.
16.1   Right on 284th St. NW (Village Rd.).
16.8   Cross 68th Ave. NW and continue straight on 284th St. NW.
18.7   Continue straight on Village Rd.

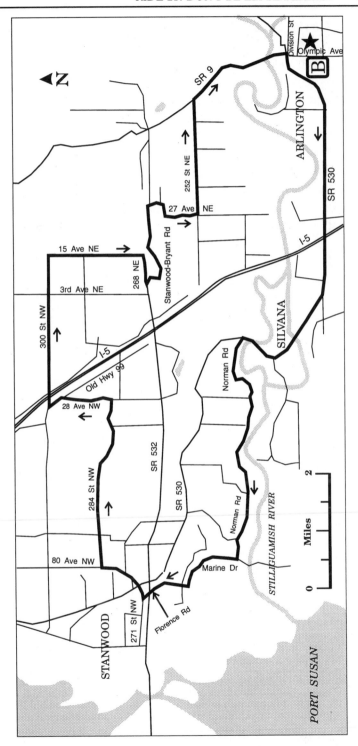

19.5   Left on 28th Ave. NW.

20.6   Left on Old Highway 99.

20.7   Right on 300th St. NW (Freeborn Rd.).

20.7   Pass under I-5.

21.8   Straight on 300th St. NW

22.9   Cross 3rd Ave. NE (Kuhnhausen Rd.) and continue straight.

23.6   Continue right on 15th Ave. NE.

25.6   Continue right on 268th St. NE (Bjordahl Rd.).

26.0   Left on Stanwood-Bryant Rd.

27.1   CAUTION! Narrow, rough, wood bridge.

27.9   Right on 27th Ave. NE (Tronson Rd.).

29.0   Left on 252nd St. NE (Kackman Rd.).

31.3   Right on SR 9.

33.5   Left on Division.

33.6   Right on Olympic Ave.

33.8   Country Bakery, Arlington.

RIDE 22

CROSS-SOUND VOYAGE

**Trips by ferry always feel like voyages to new places, even if they
are only across Puget Sound. This ride takes you to a very famous
bakery in the busy tourist town of Poulsbo in Kitsap County. You
will go up and down some of Bainbridge Island's many hills and
pause on your return at the Bainbridge Bakery in the community
of Winslow near the ferry dock. Expect great baked goods, some
main highway traffic and numerous hills.**

BAINBRIDGE BAKERY

Owner:	Hollis Faye
Address:	140 W Winslow Way, Bainbridge Island
Phone:	842-1822
Hours:	Mon-Fri 6:30am-6pm; Sat 7am-6pm; Sun 8am-5pm

Tucked away in a small shopping area in Winslow is a wonderful little
bakery. The creative juices are always at work here, devising new taste treats
for everyone who stops by.

The speciality item here is a pull-apart which is an eight grain bread
with honey and raisins made in a muffin pan and designed to separate into
four large bites. It is moist, flavorful and travels well in one's rear jersey
pocket. Another specialty is the pesto and sun-dried tomato bread. Hollis Faye
even has a unique "Bainbridge Bakery" blend of espresso and coffee
produced by Batdorf and Bronson in Olympia.

Additional items include: lemon currant scones, date walnut coffee cake,
cheddar croissant, blueberry creamcheese danish, maple walnut claws, double
chocolate pecan cookies, anise orange hazelnut bar, biscotti, rama bar (created
from left over biscotti), espresso peanut butter chip brownie, English
shortbread, fruit pies and numerous cookies.

You will find espresso, coffee, ciders, soft drinks, outdoor south-facing
seating on a large patio and friendly service.

SLUYS POULSBO BAKERY

Owners: Marion Sluys, CMB, and Daniel Sluys, CMB
Address: 18924 Front St. NE, Poulsbo
Phone: 779-2798
Hours: Mon-Sun 6:30am-6:30pm

Founded 26 years ago by Daniel Sluys, Sluys Poulsbo Bakery has become famous throughout the northwest and now the world. What made it famous is Daniel Sluys' Poulsbo bread, created from a bread recipe described in Ezkiel 4:9 of the Bible. This bread has become very popular and is now franchised even in Japan.

Daniel and his son Marion are both Certified Master Bakers (CMB) as awarded by the National Association of Retail Bakers and the first father-son pair to achieve such distinction. They both began in this location 26 years ago although the building had a bakery in it for many years before then. They have developed a reputation for producing a large variety of traditional bakery products. Although of Dutch ancestry, they have tried to provide for the tastes of this largely Scandinavian population and now even offer lefse and rosettes (egg batter deep fried in the shape of a rosette).

You cannot walk (or ride) past Sluys Bakery without stopping to gaze at the storefront window display of goodies. Once you stop, its only a few steps inside to sample whatever treat has especially caught your eye. Here you will find enough gooey pastries to fill every empty cell in your body. The Sluys serve a variety of flavored doughnuts (old fashioned, cake, applesauce, sourcream and chocolate), huge butterhorns, various flavored danish, cinnamon rounds, maple bars and Poulsbo doughnuts (square with no holes).

If you are still not satisfied, they have a whole pastry case of cookies. They produce their own fudge and almond bark and sell many types of candy including fruit slices (colored, flavored sugar jelly) and 4 oz. jaw breakers. When you have had your fill of the sweet stuff, remember their breads come in more than 30 varieties including, of course, Poulsbo bread.

You will find a large variety of sweet baked goods, free coffee, some outdoor seating on nearby benches and a waterfront park one block south.

THE RIDE

On this ride you will start with a ferry crossing (always fun) and then pedal the shores of Puget Sound on both Bainbridge Island and Liberty Bay near Poulsbo. Buy a round trip ticket and pick up a ferry schedule. Then when

Marion Sluys in his Poulsbo bakery.

you finish the ride you can hang out at the Bainbridge Bakery until the ferry comes. Just make sure you are at the bottom of the ferry dock when they are ready to load or you'll have to wait for all the cars to go ahead of you.

Start: Seattle Ferry Terminal. From I-5 take the James St. exit 164 and descend James St. to Yesler. Turn right on Yesler and park in one the pay lots near Alaskan Way. You can also find free parking south and north along Alaskan Way.

Miles: 32.3

Difficulty: Difficult. Numerous hills.

0.0	Start at Seattle Ferry Terminal. Pay at car booth and ride to front of cars -- bicycles board first.
0.2	Exit ferry. Waiting room for ferry is first building on right with restrooms. The main road climbs a hill until the first stop light.
0.4	Right on Winslow Way.
0.6	Left on Ferncliff Ave. NE.
2.3	Continue left on NE Lofgren St.
2.6	Continue right on Moran Rd. NE.
3.0	Right on Manitou Beach Dr. and keep right.
3.3	Drop down to the water with a tremendous view of the Seattle skyline and Mt. Rainier.
4.6	Right on Sunrise Dr. NE.
7.3	Faye Bainbridge State Park is on right. Steep road to sandy beach with restrooms 0.2 miles.
7.4	Continue left on NE Lafayette Ave.
7.9	Left on Euclid Ave.
8.4	Left on NE Phelps Rd.
8.5	Continue straight past the "Green Frog Rock."
8.7	Right on NE Hidden Cove Rd.
10.2	Right on SR 305 (green Bremerton sign).
11.7	Cross Agate Pass Bridge. This bridge has 2.5' sidewalks if you don't want to ride on the road surface.

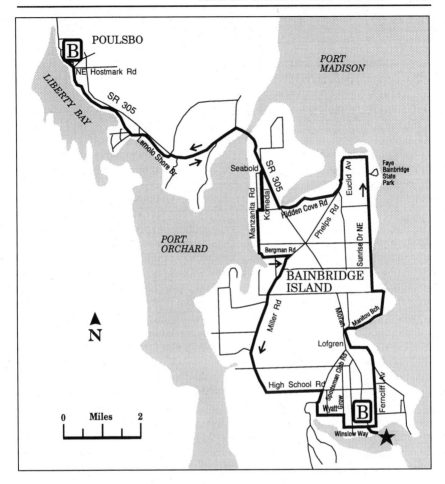

13.8 After top of long hill on main road, begin descent and turn left on Lemolo Shore Dr.

14.9 Continue right on Lemolo Shore Dr.

16.9 Left on NE Hostmark St.

17.1 Sluys Bakery is on right just before road turns left.

THE RETURN

17.1 Leave Sluys Bakery going back the way you came.

17.3 Right on Fjord Ave. NE, which turns into Lemolo Shore Dr.

20.5 Right on SR 305.

22.3 Cross Agate Pass Bridge.

23.4 Right on Seabold Rd. and immediately left on Komedal Rd. NE.

24.2 Right on NE West Hidden Cove Rd. and then left on Manzanita Rd.

25.6 Straight on NE Bergman Rd.

25.9 Right on Miller Rd.

28.9 Left on High School Rd.

30.1 Right on Sportsmans Club Rd.

30.4 Left on Finch Rd.

30.6 Left on Wyatt Way.

31.2 Right on Grow Ave. NE.

31.5 Left on Winslow Way.

31.6 Bainbridge Bakery is in the first shopping mall on your left, in the back, at the center.

32.0 Right on SR 305 downhill in right lane to the ferry.

32.3 Ferry to Seattle.

RIDE 23

DOUBLE DUTCH TREAT

**This ride takes you along a new rail-trail north out of Snohomish
and then drops down into Marysville. Here you will find the treats
offered by a Dutch couple, Gerard and Nellie Oosterwyk, born and
trained in Holland. After feasting on their wonderful baked goods,
climb back up on the plateau before dropping down to a rustic road
along the lower Snohomish River back to Snohomish.**

OOSTERWYK'S DUTCH BAKERY

Owners:	Gerard and Nellie Oosterwyk
Address:	1513 Third St., Marysville
Phone:	653-3766
Hours:	Tues-Sat 7am-5:30pm;
	closed Sunday and Monday

Welcome to a wonderful, popular bakery with traditional Dutch baking.
Here you will find a tremendous selection, a warm and bustling atmosphere,
and a dollop of the Netherlands.

Gerard Oosterwyk learned the baker's trade in his native Holland, going
through the traditional baking school programs. He worked from 1945 to
1950 for the Queen of the Netherlands. In 1956 he and his family moved to
Marysville and bought the bakery run by Carl Carlson, a Swede, who had
operated a bakery in the same building since 1921. The Oosterwyks still make
a few traditional Swedish products in honor of the original bakery.

This is a friendly, neighborhood bakery. The Oosterwyks know many of
their customers by name. It is often so busy that customers need to take a
number to get served. The walls and counters are covered with an incredible
collection of Blue Delft ceramic from Holland, all of which is available for
you to purchase.

All of the products are made from scratch. The bakery uses only
unbleached flour, no preservative and only vegetable oil. They make a few
sugarless products, but most of them are rich and sweet.

Two traditional Dutch ingredients appear in many products: almond

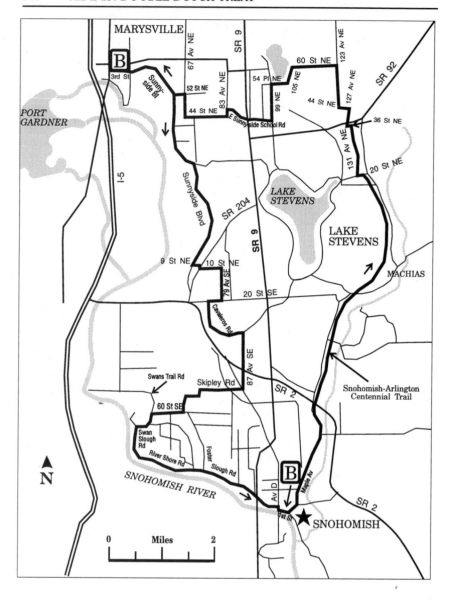

paste and currants. Examples of the Dutch treats you can sample are: Gerwilde Koek (a rich butter cookie with almond paste), Yula Kake (candied fruit and cardamom spice) and stolen made with currant bread and almond paste. You can even buy just the almond paste. Gerard and Nellie also import special Dutch treats such as Echte Goudse Stroopvafels, hard waffels made with syrup from Gouda, Netherlands.

In addition to the specialty items you will find doughnuts, cupcakes, danish, bearclaws, eclairs, applefritters, cinnamon rolls, current rolls, nut coffee cake, almond sticks, cream cheese danish, pies, double spritz cookies, nut coffee cake, date nut bread and many breads. There is ample indoor seating, self service coffee, lunch food items, restrooms, but no espresso.

THE RIDE

This is a wonderful ride which starts out on the new Snohomish-Arlington Centennial Trail (see *Washington's Rail-Trails,* by this author). You will climb gradually and then cross over a broad ridge and drop into the flatlands of the Snohomish River delta. The return ride has a steep section, then once again you drop down and ride along the Snohomish River.

Start: Sweet Life Cafe, Snohomish (see Ride 15). From I-5, take the Snohomish exit 194 right on SR 2. Turn right on the old Stevens Pass Highway that goes through Snohomish. Turn right on Ave. D and left on 1st St. The Sweet Life is at 1024 1st., #201, on the mezzanine level of the stone Marks Building. Park on the street or further east if it is full.

Miles: 37.1

Difficulty: Moderate. Some steep hills.

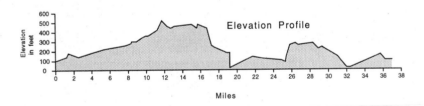

0.0   Leave the Sweet Life Cafe in Snohomish and head east.
0.1   Left on Maple Ave.
0.2   Cross 2nd St. at light. Continue north on Maple Ave.
2.5   Right into the Centennial Trail parking lot. Head north on trail.
5.3   Cross Snohomish-Machias Rd.
5.7   Machias rest area. Picnic tables, trailhead parking.
8.3   Left on 20th St. NE.
8.4   Right on 131st Ave. NE (Loth Rd.).
8.8   Intersect Hartford Rd., continue straight.
8.9   Continue straight on Old Hartford Rd.
9.5   Continue left on 36th St. NE.
9.6   Right on 127th Ave. NE (Ridel Rd.).

Cruising through the farmlands of the lower Snohomish River.

9.7 Cross SR 92. CAUTION! This is a high speed highway and there is poor visibility to your right. Cross quickly and carefully.

9.9 Left on 44th St. NE (Gregory Rd.).

10.2 Right on 123rd Ave. NE.

11.2 Left on 60th Ave. NE (Lake Cassidy Rd.).

12.3 Continue left on 105th Ave. NE.

12.7 Continue right on 54th Pl. NE.

13.1 Left on 99th Ave. NE.

14.8 Right on 42nd St. NE (E Sunnyside School Rd.).

15.3 Cross SR 9. CAUTION! Very high speed traffic.

15.6 Left on 83rd Ave. NE. (Whiskey Ridge Rd.).

15.7 Right on 44th St. NE.

16.7 Continue right on 67th Ave. NE.

17.2 Left on 52nd St. NE.

17.5 Right on Sunnyside Blvd.

18.9 Cross Liberty St. (47th Ave. NE).

19.3 Oosterwyk's Dutch Bakery is on your right at 1513 Third St.

THE RETURN

19.3 Leave Oosterwyk's Dutch Bakery and head east on Third St.

20.1 Continue straight. Third St. becomes Sunnyside Blvd.

25.4 Left on 9th St. SE.

25.5 Cross SR 204 and continue on 10th St. SE.

25.9 Right on 79th Ave. SE (Fairview Dr.).

26.5 Right on 20th St. SE (E Hewitt Ave.).

26.8 Left on Cavaleros Rd. Watch carefully for traffic coming uphill which is out of sight, then cross quickly onto Cavaleros Rd.

28.4 Right on 87th Ave. SE.

29.4 Cross Stevens Pass Highway. Turn right on 52nd St. SE (Skipley Rd.).

29.7 Continue straight on Skipley Rd. Old Fobes grocery store on corner.

31.1 Right on 60th St. SE.

31.9 Left on Homemakers Rd. (Swans Trail Rd.).

32.1 Right on Swan Slough Rd.

32.5 Left on River Shore Rd.

34.9 Right on Foster Slough Rd.

35.4 Right on 75th Ave. SE.

36.7 Right on Ave. D.

36.8 Left on 1st St.

37.1 Sweet Life Cafe, Snohomish, on your left.

RIDE 24

SWEET SNOHOMISH

This ride will take you on a reasonable route between Bothell and Snohomish. It weaves through the backroads, trying to avoid going up big hills or busy streets. However, there is still a good deal of climbing. Your rewards are some great views coming down Seattle Hill Road, a wonderful ride along the lower Snohomish River and the sweet bakery products at the Sweet Life Cafe in old town Snohomish. Stoke up for the return ride up some long hills. See Ride 15 for a description of the Sweet Life Cafe

THE RIDE

This is a popular ride from the Seattle area north to the small town of Snohomish which is fast becoming a tourist attraction based upon its antique shops. The route has some significant hills both up and down so bring high and low gears.

Start: Hillcrest Bakery, Bothell (see Ride 4). From I-5 take the Lake City Way exit 171. Follow SR 522 to Bothell. At the intersection of SR 522 and Bothell Way NE stay in the center lane and go straight onto Main St. The Hillcrest Bakery is immediately on your left. Park east on Main St. where there are no parking meters.

Miles: 40.3

Difficulty: Difficult. Some long hills.

0.0 Leave Hillcrest Bakery in Bothell and head east uphill on Main St.
1.0 Continue right on NE 195th St. crossing over I-405.
1.6 Left on 120th Ave. NE.
2.4 Left on 240th St. SE.
2.6 Right on 35th Ave. SE.

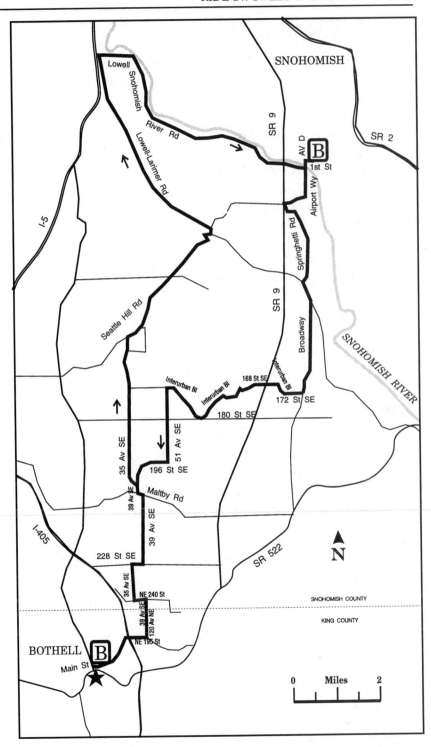

3.4   Right on 228th St. SE (Canyon Park Rd.). There is a short, steep hill on this narrow road. Use caution as you turn left just after the hill.

3.6   Left on 39th Ave. SE (Canyon Creek Rd.).

5.1   Left on Maltby Rd. This is the top of the steep climb. The church parking lot is a good place to rest and wait for your group.

5.2   Right on 38th Ave. SE.

5.3   Left on 35th Ave. SE (York Rd.).

8.6   Right on Seattle Hill Rd.

9.0   Continue left on Seattle Hill Rd.

11.4   View of Mt. Pilchuck straight ahead. Begin steep descent with tight corners and a stop sign at bottom of hill.

11.8   Left on Lowell-Larimer Rd. Continue left at the green sign pointing towards Everett.

16.7   Right on Lowell-Snohomish River Rd.

16.8   Cross two railroad tracks at the bottom of a steep hill. CAUTION! The first set of tracks has a rubber mat, the second does not and is moderately rough.

22.6   Left on Airport Way (99th Ave. SE).

22.7   Right on 1st St.

22.8   Sweet Life is on your left at 1024 1st St. in the stone Marks Building.

THE RETURN

22.8   Leave the Sweet Life behind and head west back down 1st St.

23.0   Left on Ave. D (Airport Way) and across bridge.

23.3   CAUTION! Cross two sets of **bad railroad tracks**.

24.2   Left on Springhetti Rd. The old hulk of a cedar tree on your left is the Bicycle Tree which was hollowed out early in the century for people to ride their bicycles through.

26.2   Left on Broadway.

28.1   Continue straight on Broadway. Pass the market at Cathcart.

28.7   Right on 172nd St. SE.

29.5   Right on Interurban Blvd.

29.9   Continue left on 168th St. SE.

29.5   Cross SR 9. Use caution; this is a very busy and high speed road.

30.3   Cross 73rd Ave. SE (Snohomish Ave.).

31.4   Right on 180th St. SE and take a 160 degree hard right turn onto Interurban Blvd.

32.4   Left on 51st Ave. SE.

32.9   Cross 180th St. SE.

Bicyclists below The Sweet Life Cafe.

34.0   Continue right on 196th St. SE (Jewell Rd.).

35.1   Left on Maltby Rd.

35.2   Right on 39th Ave. SE.

36.7   Right on 228th St. SE.

37.0   Left on 35th Ave. SE.

37.7   Left on 240th St. SE.

38.0   Right on 39th Ave. SE (becomes 120th Ave. NE).

38.8   Right on NE 195th St.

39.9   Cross I-405 and keep left.

40.3   Hillcrest Bakery, Bothell.

RIDE 25

HISTORIC BLACK DIAMOND

Black Diamond was a major city at the turn of the century, nestled in the heart of the area's coal mines. This ride takes you up a long hill to reach a bakery started way back in 1902 that has changed in some, but not all ways. If you pick a day with clear skies you will be rewarded with great views of Mt. Rainier and the Green River Gorge.

BLACK DIAMOND BAKERY

Owner: Doug Weiding
Address: 32805 Railroad Ave., Black Diamond
Phone: 886-2741
Hours: Mon-Fri 7am-4pm; Sat-Sun 7am-5pm

This is an historic bakery that has been around since 1902. The name Black Diamond comes from the nickname for the coal found in the area. The mines near Black Diamond were some of the largest producing coal mines in the region. Just north down the street is a wonderful railroad/history museum open Saturdays which is well worth the visit.

There is living history right in the Black Diamond Bakery. Doug Weiding continues to use a traditional, and perhaps unique, process to produce his wonderful baked products. Not only is his a wood fired oven, the wood is actually placed in the baking chamber, fired to generate the proper temperature, then removed so the bread and pastries can be put right in its place to bake. Every afternoon a half cord of wood is loaded into the cooking area and lit. At three the next morning, the ashes are removed, the cooking stones washed and the bread placed on the hot stones. The trick for the bakers is that the temperature of the oven varies considerably requiring careful attention to baking times. If you want, you can get a free tour of the oven.

From this oven come wonderful breads with more than 26 varieties to choose from. The best pastry product is the cinnamon roll, once voted by radio listeners as the best in the region. They also produce doughnuts, apple fritters, turnovers, blueberry muffins and other pastries. They have chocolates, hard candy, ice cream cones, espresso and coffee.

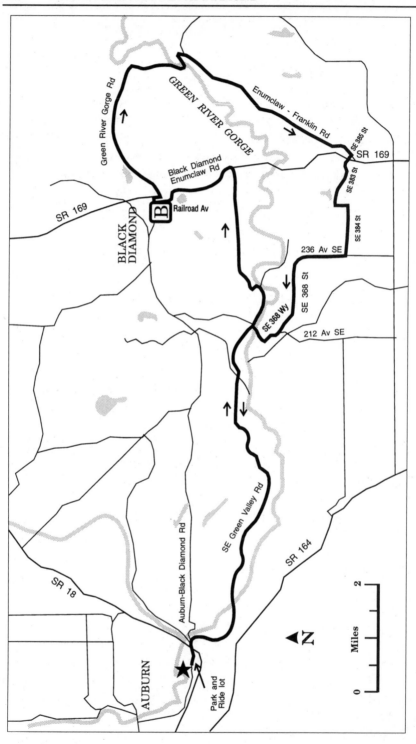

The bakery has been upgraded in recent years to include a large deli area serving breakfast and lunch. The room has a direct view of Mt. Rainier through a floor to ceiling glass wall. You will find inside seating, restrooms and plenty of rich food.

THE RIDE

This is a delightful ride up the quiet lower Green River Valley, up a long steep hill, across a high bridge over the upper Green River Gorge, across the flat Enumclaw Plateau and dropping down into the lower Green River Valley again. Bring some low gears and a good appetite.

Start: Auburn. From I-5 take the Auburn exit 142. Follow SR 18 east to the Green River Valley exit. Turn left and take the Auburn Black Diamond Rd. west 0.2 miles and turn left in Metro's gravel Park and Ride lot. Park here.

Miles: 34.3

Difficulty: Difficult. One long steep hill.

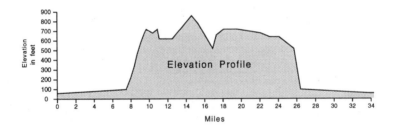

0.0   Metro Park and Ride. Turn right onto Auburn Black Diamond Rd.

0.2   Right on SE Green Valley Rd.

0.6   Pass Green Valley Meats & Mini Market on right.

7.5   Pass Whitney Bridge King County Park.

8.0   Begin uphill climb. The turnoff to Flaming Geyser State Park is on the right. CAUTION! This is a long, steep hill. Be prepared for cars coming up from behind not seeing you on right hand corners.

10.9   Left on Black Diamond Enumclaw Rd.

11.1   Left on Jones Lake Rd. (Railroad Ave.). You will see this road is part way uphill on your left.

12.5   Black Diamond Bakery is on your left.

THE RETURN

12.5   Leave the Black Diamond Bakery and continue north.

12.6   Take first right going uphill (Baker St.).

12.7   Right on SR 169 and immediately take the first left onto Green River Gorge Rd. (Lawson St.).

16.8   Franklin Bridge over the Green River Gorge. Franklin is the name for the former mining town behind you on your right.

16.9   Green River Gorge Resort. A private resort that has private trails down into the gorge.

17.3   Continue straight on the Enumclaw-Franklin Rd.

21.1   Right on SE 385th St. Go 100 yards and cross Enumclaw-Black Diamond Rd.

21.2   Continue on SE 383rd St. (It winds around and becomes SE 384th St.)

23.3   Right on 236th Ave. SE.

23.8   Continue left on SE 368th St. (E Whitney Hill Rd.).

24.3   Continue right on SE 368th Way.

25.7   Right on 212th Ave. SE.

26.4   Left on SE Green Valley Rd.

33.8   Left on Auburn Black Diamond Rd.

34.3   Left into Metro Park & Ride lot.

RIDE 26

MT. RAINIER VISTAS

The Enumclaw Plateau is a great place to bicycle. It is primarily flat, has several quiet side roads and when it is clear provides breath-taking views of Mt. Rainier. This route starts at the old community of Georgetown near Ravensdale east of Kent and loops down and around Enumclaw. Except on Fridays and Saturdays you can stop into an unusually healthy food store with great pastries and breads, the Rainier Natural Food Store and Bakery.

RAINIER NATURAL FOOD STORE & BAKERY

Owners:	Ray and Gloria Huber
Address:	38629 Auburn-Enumclaw Rd., Auburn
Phone:	833-4369
Hours:	Mon-Thurs 9am-6pm; Sun 9am-3pm;
	closed Friday and Saturday

The Rainier Natural Food Store and Bakery is a health food grocery which produces some of the best quality bread around. Ray and Gloria Huber specialize in sprouted grain breads made by carefully mixing the grains together, soaking them in well water until they sprout and then grinding them directly into bread dough while still wet. This process produces high protein, high gluten breads which go off the FDA charts. The wheat used comes from Three Forks, Montana, and is a hard red winter variety. You will find Rainier Natural Food breads in the Puget Sound Co-ops and many health food stores in the region.

The Hubers have been bakers for many years and took over this bakery eleven years ago. They are very knowledgeable about bread products and have unusual ones like their spelt grain bread. Spelt grain is low in gluten, which is the part of wheat which some people are allergic to. They also have teff flour, a very fine seed which is used in Ethiopian breads and pancakes.

In addition to breads, Rainier Natural Foods offers several tasty treats. Especially full of energy for bicyclists are the peanut bars which are rich, very peanuty and have a swirl of chocolate inside. There are cinnamon rolls and healthy drinks and juices and cookies made with carob chips instead of

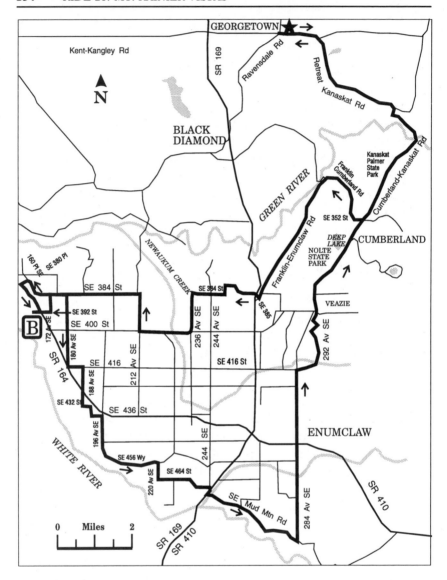

chocolate. The Hubers produce sugar free apple and blueberry single-serving pies and muffins. There are also three cookies that are wheat free; rice carob brownie, rice oatmeal and rice spice coconut. The only white sugar used is for the icing on the cinnamon rolls.

You will find assorted baked goods, grocery items, books, cold drinks and many breads.

THE RIDE

This is a long, flat ride around the Enumclaw plateau. In good weather you will have tremendous vistas of Mt. Rainier everywhere you turn.

Start: Georgetown (east of Kent). From I-5 take the Auburn exit 142 and follow SR 18 east past Auburn. From SR 18 take the SE 272nd St. (SR 516) exit and follow the Kent-Kangley Rd. heading east to Georgetown.

Miles: 56.2

Difficulty: Difficult. No steep hills but long distance and a high speed highway crossing.

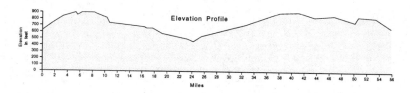

Shortcut: Start and finish at Cumberland. This makes the ride 39.4 miles total.

0.0   Start at Georgetown Market, at the corner of the Kent-Kangley Rd. and Ravensdale Way. Head east on Kent-Kangley Rd.

1.1   Right on Retreat-Kanaskat Rd.

5.2   Right on Cumberland-Kanaskat Rd. over railroad tracks.

5.5   Cross the Green River Gorge.

6.2   Pass Kanaskat-Palmer State Park on right. Steep paved road down to picnic area and restrooms along Green River, 0.3 miles.

8.4   Right on SE 352nd St. The Cumberland Store is 0.1 miles ahead of you on the left .

8.6   Continue right on Franklin-Cumberland Rd.

10.6   Left on Franklin-Enumclaw Rd. The Franklin Bridge over the Green River is to your right 0.2 miles.

14.5   Right on SE 385th St.

14.6   Cross SR 169 and continue straight on SE 383rd St. which winds around and turns into SE 384th St.

16.3   Cross 244th Ave. SE.

16.8   Left on 236th Ave. SE.

Mark, Laurie and Melissa enjoying a country ride near Enumclaw.

17.7   Right on SE 400th St.
19.2   Right on 212th Ave. SE.
20.2   Continue left on SE 384th St.
23.2   Continue right on 160th Pl. SE.
23.5   Left on SE 380th Pl.
23.6   Left on SR 164.
24.2   Right at Rainier Natural Food Store and Bakery.

THE RETURN

24.2   Leave Rainier Natural Food Store and Bakery. Turn right on SR 169.
24.7   Left on SE 392nd St.
25.0   Continue left on 172nd Ave. SE.
25.5   Right on SE 384th St.
26.0   Right on 180th Ave. SE.
27.0   Cross SE 400th St. and continue straight on 180th Ave. SE.
28.0   Left on SE 416th St.
28.5   Right on 188th Ave. SE.

29.2   Cross SR 169 and continue straight on 188th Ave. SE.

29.6   Left on SE 432nd St.

29.9   Continue right on 192nd Ave. SE.

30.1   Continue left on SE 436th St.

30.3   Right on 196th Ave. SE.

31.1   Continue left on SE 456th Way.

32.6   Right on 220th Ave. SE.

32.9   Continue left on SE 464th St.

34.0   Continue right on SE 468th Way.

34.4   Continue left on SE 468th St.

34.7   Right on 244th Ave. SE.

34.8   Right on SR 410. CAUTION! Carefully get in left part of lane and turn quickly but cautiously at next left in 400 yards (SE Mud Mountain Rd.). Do not stop in the lane and do not do this in a large group!

35.0   Left on SE Mud Mountain Rd.

38.2   Left on 284th Ave. SE.

40.7   Cross SR 410 and continue straight on 284th Ave. SE.

42.8   Right on SE 416th St. and continue north.

44.8   Left on 292nd Ave. SE. and right on Veazie-Cumberland Rd.

46.3   Nolte State Park is on your left. Swimming lake, restrooms.

47.5   Cumberland Grocery.

50.1   Kanaskat-Palmer State Park is on your left.

51.9   Left on Retreat-Kanaskat Rd.

55.1   Left on Kent-Kangley Rd.

56.2   Georgetown Market.

RIDE 27

OVER THE HILL

This ride connects Arlington and Mt. Vernon via a very scenic, although sometimes hilly, route. You will travel up Highway 9 north of Arlington through the deep woods, climb over Little Mountain and drop onto the flats of Mt. Vernon. After feasting at the City Bakery, if you can still ride, you will cruise along the Skagit River and then climb the start of the foothills back over to Arlington via some very wooded back roads.

CITY BAKERY

Owners:	Jim and Pat Grenfeld
Address:	514 S 1st St., Mt. Vernon
Phone:	336-3001
Hours:	Mon-Fri 7am-5:30pm; Sat 7am-5pm; **closed Sunday**

Located in the heart of downtown Mt. Vernon, this is a large, open bakery with plenty of goodies and plenty of places to sit and relax. The Grenfelds continue a 75 year old tradition of fine baking in Mt. Vernon. The original bakery was located down the street in the President Hotel and had a wood fired oven with a brick front. When the bakery moved to its present location, the Grenfeld's did it in traditional small-town style -- they hosted a parade down main street with all the parts of the oven and other bakery machines being carried by the townspeople.

The wood-fired oven is gone, but the delicious baked goods continue. At the City Bakery you will find pies, cakes, cookies, chocolates, pastries and croissants. Unusual items are "mountains", peaks of coconut dipped in chocolate, Swedish "tosca", almond cake dipped in almond sauce, and frugiassa, a flat bread filled with spicy vegtables. The Grenfelds also produce some seasonal favorites such as gingerbread houses and tulip cookies (they look like tulips). Carrying on a tradition of the former bakers, they still make their own chocolates and truffles. Specialties include rolls filled with sausage or vegetables.

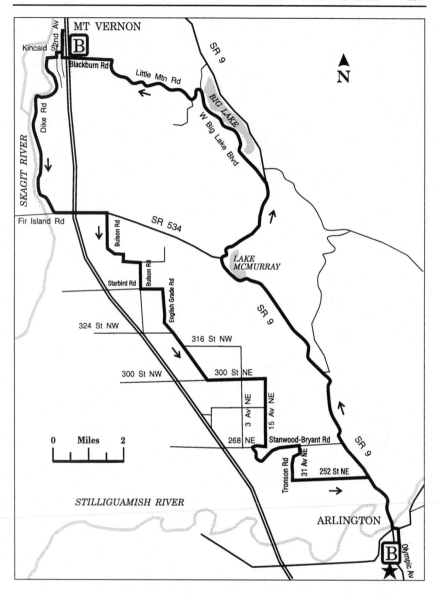

The City Bakery has a substantial lunch service with fresh roasted turkey, roast beef and ham sandwiches, and beatles (egg dough pocket sandwiches). You will find soups, salads, self service soft drinks, inside seating and restrooms. There is a bike rack next door and a bike shop, Cascade Sports, across the street.

THE RIDE

This is a long, hilly ride through some very rural country. Be prepared for some traffic on SR 9 and a very tough hill from Lake McMurray over the top to Mt. Vernon.

Start: Country Bakery, Arlington (see Ride 19). From I-5, take the northern Arlington exit 208. Follow SR 530 east into Arlington and turn right on Olympic Ave. Park in front of the bakery or one block east on the street. You can also park at Haller Park located 0.3 miles north on SR 9 just before the bridge over the Stillaguamish River.

Miles: 51.7

Difficulty: Difficult. Long with steep hills.

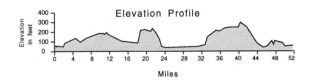

0.0   Start at the Country Bakery, Arlington. Go north on Olympic Ave.

0.2   Turn left on Division St. and immediately turn right on Highway 9.

0.5   Pass Haller Park on your left. Restrooms, river access, picnic benches.

0.6   CAUTION! Cross Stillaguamish River on a narrow bridge.

5.6   Narrow bridge just after a left corner. Use caution.

10.7 Lake McMurray Store.

10.9 Continue straight on SR 9.

14.6 Left on W Big Lake Rd.

18.1 Left on Little Mtn. Rd.

18.6 Continue right on Little Mtn. Rd.

21.8 Left on Blackburn Rd.

23.2 Right on S 2nd St. after crossing two railroad tracks with rubber mats.

24.0 Left on Kincaid St. at stop light then right on S 1st St.

24.2 City Bakery is on your right halfway down S 1st St. at 514 S 1st St. Cascade Sports is across the street.

THE RETURN

24.2 Leave the City Bakery and head south back down S 1st St.

24.8 Right on Hazel St.

25.3 Right on Dike Rd.

31.1 Left at stop sign onto Fir Island Rd. (unmarked).

31.3 Cross two sets of railroad tracks. Note the inside lane is the only one with rubber mats.

32.7 Right on Bulson Rd. which winds around going uphill. You will come to a dead end sign on Tyee Rd. Turn right and continue on Bulson Rd.

35.8 Left on Starbird Rd.

36.6 Continue right on Starbird Rd. (English Grade Rd.).

38.0 Cross 324th St. NW.

39.8 Left on 300th St. NW.

40.9 Cross 3rd Ave. NE.

41.7 Right on 15th Ave. NE.

43.7 Continue right on 268th St. NE.

44.1 Left on Stanwood-Bryant Rd.

45.2 CAUTION! Narrow rough wooden bridge. Access to Pilchuck Creek.

46.0 Right on Tronson Rd. (31st Ave. NE).

47.1 Left on 252nd St. NE (Kackman Rd.).

49.4 Right on SR 9.

51.6 Left on Division St.

51.7 Right on Olympic Ave.

APPENDIX A

BAKERIES

A La Francaise

Location: University Village Shopping Center, Seattle
Owner: Joan Johnson
Address: 2609 NE University Village Shopping Center, Seattle
Phone: 524-9300
Hours: M-F 7:30am-8pm; Sat-Sun 7:30am-6pm
Rides: 4 and 10
Directions: From I-5 take the NE 45th St. exit (Exit 169). Turn right (east) past the University of Washington campus, to the base of long, steep hill. Turn right before you reach the bottom at sign for 25th Ave NE. Take an immediate right into University Village Shopping Center and take the first left. A La Francaise is on your right in the courtyard.

A Piece of Cake

Location: International District, Seattle
Owner: Mr. Basil
Manager: Amy Lou
Address: 514 S King St., Seattle
Phone: 623-8284
Hours: Mon-Fri 9am-7pm; Sat-Sun 10am-7pm
Ride: 7
Directions: From I-5, take the James St. exit 165. Turn west (downhill) and turn left (south) on 5th Ave. Go across S Jackson and turn left on King St.

Alki Bakery

Location: Alki Neighborhood, Seattle
Owner: Kevin Piper
Address: 2738 Alki Ave. SW, Seattle
Phone: 935-0616
Hours: Sun-Thurs 8am-9:30am; Fri-Sat 8am-10pm
Ride: 5
Directions: From I-5 take the Spokane St. exit 163(a) and head west. Take the Harbor Ave. SW exit and continue along Harbor Ave. SW. It becomes Alki Ave. SW and the Alki Bakery is at 2738 Alki Ave. SW.

Bainbridge Bakery

Location: Winslow, Bainbridge Island
Owner: Hollis Faye
Address: 140 Winslow Way, Bainbridge Island
Phone: 842-1822
Hours: Mon-Fri 6:30am-6pm; Sat 7am-6pm; Sun 8am-5pm
Rides: 22
Directions: From the downtown Seattle ferry terminal, take the ferry to Bainbridge Island. Depart and take the first left on Winslow Way. The Bainbridge Bakery is located in the last shopping mall on your right, in the center, at the back.

Baker's Beach Cafe

Location: Mt. Baker Neighborhood, Seattle
Owners: Patience Cryst and Lenard Yen
Location: 3601 S McClellan St., Seattle
Phone: 725-3654
Hours: Mon-Fri 6:30am-9pm; Sat-Sun 7am-3pm
Rides: 8 and 10
Directions: From I-5 take I-520 east and take the Montlake Blvd. exit. Go straight across Montlake Blvd. and continue on Lake Washington Boulevard to Leshi. Continue on Lake St. under I-90 and take a right on Lake Park Dr. S. Baker's Beach Cafe is straight ahead and a little to your right on the corner of S McClellan St. and Lake Park Dr. S.

Ballard Baking Company

Location: Ballard Neighborhood, Seattle
Owners: Mark and Marja Handman
Address: 5909 24th Ave. NW, Seattle
Phone: 781-0091
Hours: Tues-Sat 7am-7pm; Sun 7am-5pm; **closed Monday**
Ride: 6
Directions: From I-5, take the NE 45th St. exit 169. Follow NE 45th St. west onto Market St. in Ballard. Turn right on 24th Ave NW. Ballard Baking Company is on your left.

Black Diamond Bakery

Location: Black Diamond
Owner: Doug Weiding
Address: 32805 Railroad Ave., Black Diamond
Phone: 886-2741
Hours: Mon-Fri 7am-4pm; Sat-Sun 7am-5pm
Ride: 25
Directions: From I-5 go east on I-405 and take the SR 169 exit to Maple Valley. Continue south on SR 169 to Black Diamond. Turn right on Baker St. and left on Railroad Ave. to the bakery.

Blake's Bakery

Location: West Seattle Neighborhood, Seattle
Owner: Hanna Yuse
Address: 4737 California Ave. SW, Seattle
Phone: 937-4554
Hours: Tues-Sat 6:30am-6pm; **closed Sunday and Monday**
Ride: 5
Directions: From I-5 take the Spokane St. exit 163(a) and follow Fauntleroy Way. Turn right on SW Alaska St. and left on California Ave SW. Blake's Bakery is in the first block, on your right.

Bob's Bakery

Location: Vashon Center, Vashon Island
Owner: Bob Long
Address: 17506 Vashon Highway SW, Vashon
Phone: 463-5666
Hours: Tues-Fri 7am-6pm; Sat 9am-5pm;
                 closed Sunday and Monday
Ride: 20
Directions: From I-5 take the Spokane Street exit 163(a) and follow Fauntleroy Way to the Fauntleroy ferry terminal. Take the Vashon ferry to Vashon Island and stay on Vashon Highway SW 4.7 miles south.

Boulangerie

Location: Wallingford Neighborhood, Seattle
Manager: Marian Dam
Address: 2200 N 45th St., Seattle
Phone: 634-2211
Hours: Mon-Sun 7am-7pm
Ride: 6
Directions: From I-5 take the NE 45th St. exit 169 and head west. Boulangerie is one mile west.

Brusseau's in Edmonds

Location: Edmonds
Owner: William Keegan
Address: 115 5th Ave. S, Edmonds
Phone: 774-4166
Hours: Mon-Fri 7am-5pm; Sat-Sun 8am-5pm
Ride: 9
Directions: From I-5, take the Edmonds exit 177 and head west on SR 104. Take the 5th Ave. exit and Brusseau's is located one block before the traffic circle in the center of Edmonds.

Calico Cupboard, The

Location: LaConner
Owner: Linda Freed
Address: 720 First St., LaConner
Phone: 466-4451
Hours: Mon-Fri 7:30am-5pm; Sat-Sun 7:30am-5pm
Ride: 18
Directions: From I-5 take the Conway exit 221. Go west over the freeway and take the first right on Fir Island Rd. Follow the signs to LaConner.

City Bakery

Location: Mt. Vernon
Owners: Jim and Pat Grenfeld
Address: 514 S First St., Mt. Vernon
Phone: 336-3001
Hours: Mon-Fri 7am-5:30pm; Sat 7am-5pm; **closed Sunday**
Ride: 27
Directions: From I-5 take the Mt. Vernon exit 226. Turn left (west) under the freeway and turn right on First St.

Cornerstone Desserts & Espresso

Location: Redmond
Owner: Sam Strok
Address: 16315 Cleveland St. NE, Redmond
Phone: 883-3871
Hours: Mon-Fri 6:30am-7pm; Sat-Sun 7:30-6pm
Ride: 2
Directions: From I-5 take I-520 east towards Redmond. Take the West Lake Sammamish exit and turn left on SR 920. Take the first right onto Leary Way. Go across the railroad tracks and take the first right on Cleveland St. NE. The Cornerstone is immediately on your right.

Country Bakery, The

Location: Arlington
Owner: Dennis Jarman
Address: 324 Olympic Ave., Arlington
Phone: 453-2866
Hours: Tues-Sat 6:30am-5pm; **closed Sunday and Monday**
Rides: 19, 21 and 27
Directions: From I-5 take the Arlington exit 208. Turn right (east) on SR 530 and turn right again on Olympic Ave.

Crawford's Bakery Cafe Company

Location: Bellevue
Owners: Michael and Alexis Petrone
Address: 10246A Main St., Bellevue
Phone: 451-3761
Hours: Mon-Sat 7am-6pm; Sun 7am-1pm
Ride: 10
Directions: From I-5 take I-520 to I-405. Head towards Bellevue and take the SE 4th St. exit, turn right on SE 4th St., right on 112th Ave. SE, and left on Main St. Head west across Bellevue Way and the bakery is on Main St. in old Bellevue on your right.

Daily Grind

Location: Montlake Neighborhood, Seattle
Owner: Jackson Cremer
Address: 2301 24th Ave. E, Seattle
Phone: 322-9885
Hours: Mon-Sun 4am-2pm
Rides: 8 and 10
Directions: From I-5 take I-520 eastbound and take the Montlake Blvd. exit. Turn right on Montlake Pl. E. and continue seven blocks south to E Lynn St.

PLEASE ORDER YOUR HOLIDAY PIES E
APPLE, APPLE-CRANBERRY, BANANA
BLUEBERRY, CHERRY, CHOCOLATE
CUSTARD, COCONUT CUSTARD, LE
LEMON MERINGUE, AND PUMPKIN
ALSO AVAILABLE: HOLIDAY CAKES AND

Michael Petrone of Crawford's Bakery Cafe Company.

Dulce's Bakery and Cafe

Location: Alki,Neighborhood, West Seattle
Owners: Carlos Kainz and Julie Juerrero
Address: 4100 Beach Dr. SW, Seattle
Phone: 933-8400
Hours: Tues-Wed 7am-6pm; Thurs-Sat 7am-9pm; Sun 7am-3pm;
                 closed Monday
Ride: 5
Directions: From I-5 take the Spokane St. exit 163(a) and head west. Take the Harbor Ave. SW exit and continue along Harbor Ave. SW which turns into Alki Ave. SW. Turn left on 63rd Ave. SW and left again on Beach Dr. SW.

Exquisite Desserts

Location: Madison Neighborhood, Seattle
Owners: Debby Egger and Patty Sullivan
Address: 2800 E Madison St., Seattle
Phone: 328-0518
Hours: Mon-Fri 7:30am-6pm; Sat-Sun 8:30am-5pm
Rides: 8 and 10
Directions: From I-5 take I-520 east and take the Montlake Blvd. exit. Go straight across Montlake Blvd. and continue on Lake Washington Boulevard to E Madison St. Turn right on E Madison. Exquisite Desserts is on the corner of E Madison and 28th Ave. E.

French Pastry Place, Ltd., The

Location: Mercer Island
Owners: Jean-Claude Ferre and LeeAnn Belarde
Address: 7695 SE 27th St., Mercer Island
Phone: 236-1727
Hours: Mon-Thurs 7am-6:30pm; Fri 7am-7pm; Sat 8am-5pm;
                 Sun 8am-3pm
Ride: 10
Directions: From I-90 heading east from Seattle, take exit 6B, 76th Ave. Turn right and then left on SE 27th. The French Pastry Place, Ltd. is on the right at the end of the block.

Frombach's Old Home Bakery

Location: West Seattle
Owner: Joe McKuen
Address: 2332 California Ave. SW, Seattle
Phone: 932-5574
Hours: Mon-Fri 6am-6pm; Sat 6:30am-5pm; Sun 7am-1pm
Ride: 5
Directions: From I-5 take the Spokane St. exit 163(a) and follow Fauntleroy Way. Turn right on SW Alaska St. and right again on California Ave. SW. Go two miles north on California Ave. SW.

George's Bakery

Location: North Bend
Owners: Greg and Cornelia Cordova
Address: 127 North Bend Way, North Bend
Phone: 888-0632
Hours: Tues-Fri 6:30am-6pm; Sat 7:30am-6pm;
        Sun 8:30:am-5:00pm; **closed Monday**
Ride: 16
Directions: From I-5 take I-90 eastbound to the North Bend exit 32. Go north under the freeway and turn right in town on North Bend Way. George's Bakery is in the first block on your right.

Grand Central Bakery

Location: Grand Central Arcade, Pioneer Square, Seattle
Owner: Gwenyth Basseti
Address: 214 1st Ave. S, Seattle
Phone: 622-3644
Hours: Mon-Fri 7am-6pm; Sat-Sun 9am-5pm
Ride: 7
Directions: From I-5, take the James St. exit 165. Turn west (downhill) and turn left (south) on 1st Ave. Cross Yesler Way and look for the Grand Central sign over a large stone building on the corner of Main St. and 1st Ave. S.

Great Harvest Bread Co.

Location: Lake Forest Park Neighborhood, Seattle
Owners: Jeff and Maggy Weisman
Address: 171 Bothell Way NE, Seattle
Phone: 365-4778
Hours: Mon-Fri 7am-9pm; Sat-Sun 7am-6pm
Rides: 8 and 10
Directions: From I-5 take the Lake City Way exit 171 and follow SR 522 through Lake City to the bottom of a long hill. Turn left at the traffic light on NE 170th Ave. and enter the Lake Forest Park Towne Centre. The bakery is straight back in the center of the shopping mall.

Greenwood Bakery Cafe

Location: Greenwood Neighborhood, Seattle
Owners: Mark and Marja Handman
Address: 7227 Greenwood Ave. N, Seattle
Phone: 783-7181
Hours: Tues-Sat 6:30am-9pm; Sun 7am-1pm; **closed Monday**
Ride: 6
Directions: From I-5 take the 50th Street exit 169 and head west. Continue west under Aurora Ave. N. to Phinney Ave. N. Continue right on Phinney Ave. N. which winds over to Greenwood Ave. N. Look for a large blue canopy that says Ken's Market at N 73rd St. The Greenwood Bakery is next door.

Hillcrest Bakery

Location: Bothell
Owners: Lyda, Peter and Bob Kaskes
Address: 10010 Main St., Bothell
Phone: 486-5292
Hours: Mon-Fri 6am-6pm; Sat 6am-5pm; **closed Sunday**
Rides: 2 and 4
Directions: From I-5 take the Lake City Way exit 171 and follow SR 522 to Bothell. In Bothell, stay in the left lane and go straight at 10th Ave. NE onto Main St. The bakery is immediately on your left.

Honeybear Bakery

Location: Wallingford Neighborhood, Seattle
Owners: Carl Gaskill and Rissa Warner
Address: 2106 N 55th St., Seattle
Phone: 545-7296
Hours: Mon-Sun 6am-11pm
Ride: 6
Directions: From I-5 take the NE 45th St. exit 169 and head west. Turn right on Meridian Ave. N. and continue straight to N 55th St.

Langley Village Bakery

Location: Langley, Whidbey Island
Owner: Marie Bird-Legters
Address: 227 2nd St., Langley
Phone: 221-3133
Hours: Mon-Sat 7:30am-5pm; Sun 8:30am-2:30pm
Ride: 13
Directions: From I-5 take the Mukilteo exit 182 westbound to the ferry terminal at Mukilteo. Take the ferry across Puget Sound to Clinton. Take the main highway, SR 525, west to Langley Rd. Turn right on Langley Rd. and left onto 2nd St. in Langley.

Le Panier Very French Bakery

Location: Pike Place Market, Seattle
Owner: Hubert Loevenbruck
Manager: Kimberly A. Wiganosky
Address: 1902 Pike Place, Seattle
Phone: 441-3669
Hours: Mon-Sat 7am-6:30pm; **closed Sunday**
Ride: 7
Directions: From I-5 take the Stewart St. exit 167. Go straight to Pike Place.

McGraw St. Bakery

Location: Queen Anne Neighborhood, Seattle
Owner: Jessica Reisam
Address: 615 W McGraw St., Seattle
Phone: 284-6327
Hours: Mon-Fri 7am-6pm; Sat-Sun 8am-6pm
Ride: 1
Directions: From I-5 take the NE 45th St. exit 169 and head west on NE 45th St. Turn left onto Aurora Ave. N. (SR 99) and right on Queen Anne Way N at the south end of the Aurora Bridge. Go straight through the first stop sign, left on Queen Anne Ave. N. and right on McGraw St.

Oosterwyk's Dutch Bakery

Location: Marysville
Owners: Gerard and Nellie Oosterwyk
Address: 1513 Third St., Marysville
Phone: 653-3766
Hours: Tues-Sat 7am-5:30pm; **closed Sunday and Monday**
Ride: 23
Directions: From I-5 take the Marysville exit 199. Turn right (east) and then right onto State Ave. Take the next left on 3rd St.

Original Bakery, The

Location: Fauntleroy Neighborhood, Seattle
Owner: Bernie Alonzo
Address: 9253 45th Ave. SW, Seattle
Phone: 938-5088
Hours: Tues-Fri 7:30am-6pm; Sat 7:30am-5pm; Sun 8am-4pm;
             closed Monday
Ride: 20
Directions: From I-5 take the Spokane Street exit 163(a) and follow Fauntleroy Way to the Fauntleroy ferry terminal. Continue past the ferry terminal and turn left on Wildwood Place. The bakery is in the small cluster of buildings at Wildwood Place and 45th Ave. SW.

Original Brown Bag Cafe & Bakery, The

Location: Carnation
Owner: Alex Awasthi
Address: 4366 Tolt Ave., Carnation
Phone: 333-6100
Hours: Mon-Sun 6:30am-3pm
Ride: 11
Directions: From I-5 take I-90 east to the Preston exit 22. Turn left (north) and take the first right onto Preston-Fall City Rd. SE and follow it to Fall City. Go right across the bridge over the Snoqualmie River and immediately left on SR 203 to Carnation.

Pert's, A Deli on Leschi

Location: Leshi Neighborhood, Seattle
Owners: Sue Pert and Gaye Ishimaru
Address: 120 Lakeside Ave., Seattle
Phone: 325-0277
Hours: Mon-Sat 8am-4pm; Sun 8am-2pm
Rides: 8 and 10
Directions: From I-5 take I-520 east and take the Montlake Blvd. exit. Go straight across Montlake Blvd. and continue on Lake Washington Boulevard to Leshi.

Piroshky, Piroshky

Location: Pike Place Market, Seattle
Owners: Zina and Vladimir Kotelnikov
Address: 1908 Pike Place, Seattle
Phone: 441-6068
Hours: Mon-Sun 9am-5pm
Ride: 7
Directions: From I-5 take the Stewart St. exit 167. Go straight to Pike Place.

Rainier Natural Food Store and Bakery

Location:	Auburn-Enumclaw Rd.
Owners:	Ray and Gloria Huber
Address:	38629 Auburn-Enumclaw Rd, Auburn
Phone:	833-4369
Hours:	Mon-Thurs 9am-6pm; Sun 9am-3pm; **closed Friday and Saturday**
Ride:	26

Directions: From I-5 take the Auburn exit 142 east onto SR 18. Turn off SR 18 onto SR 410, the Auburn-Enumclaw Rd. just beyond SE 380th Pl. Rainier Natural Food Store and Bakery is the large building on the right.

Scandia Bakery and Lefse Factory

Location:	Stanwood
Owners:	Don Haugon and Ken Turner
Address:	8706 271st St. NW, Stanwood
Phone:	629-2411
Hours:	Tues-Sat 8am-5pm; **closed Sunday and Monday**
Ride:	21

Directions: From I-5 take the Stanwood exit 212 and head west on SR 532. The Scandia Bakery and Lefse Factory is downtown on the south side of 271st St. NW, the main street through town.

Sky River Bakery

Location:	Monroe
Owners:	Karen Clifton, Mary Thorgerson and Andrew Abt
Address:	117 1/2 Main St., Monroe
Phone:	794-7434
Hours:	Tues-Fri 7am-5pm; Sat 7am-4pm; **closed Sunday and Monday**
Rides:	12, 15 and 17

Directions: From I-5 take I-520 east to I-405 and head north. Take the Monroe exit 23 from I-405 and head east on SR 522 to Monroe. From SR 522 turn left onto SR 2 and right onto Lewis St. Turn right on Main St. and the bakery is on the right towards the end of the block.

Sluys Poulsbo Bakery

Location:	Poulsbo
Owners:	Marion Sluys, CMB, and Daniel Sluys, CMB
Address:	18924 Front St. NE, Poulsbo
Phone:	779-2798
Hours:	Mon-Sun 6:30am-6:30pm
Ride:	22

Directions: From the downtown Seattle ferry terminal take the ferry to Bainbridge Island. Depart the ferry and head west on SR 305. Turn left on Lincoln Rd. at the green sign that says Poulsbo. The bakery is in the middle of town where the main road takes a slight jog.

Still Life in Fremont Coffeehouse

Location:	Fremont Neighborhood, Seattle
Owners:	Nancy Weintraub and Ruth Quinet
Address:	709 N 35th St., Seattle
Phone:	547-9850
Hours:	Sun-Thurs 7:30am-9pm; Fri-Sat 8am-5pm; Sun 8am-12noon
Rides:	4 and 6

Directions: From I-5 take the NE 45th St. exit 169 and go west. Turn left on Stone Way N. and right on N 35th St.

Stoll's Madison Park Bakery

Location:	Madison Park Neighborhood, Seattle
Owner:	Fred Stoll
Address:	4214 E Madison St., Seattle
Phone:	322-3238
Hours:	Tues-Fri 7am-6:30pm; Sat 7am-5:30pm; **closed Sunday and Monday**
Rides:	8 and 10

Directions: From I-5 take the Madison St. exit 165. Head east up a very steep hill and turn left onto Terry Ave. Turn right on Madison and follow it all the way to the Madison Park neighborhood near Lake Washington.

Store Next Door, The

Location: Wallingford Neighborhood, Seattle
Owner: Julia Miller
Address: 4405 Wallingford Ave., Seattle
Phone: 547-3203
Hours: Mon-Fri 7am-6pm; Sat 8am-5pm; Sun 8am-12noon
Ride: 6
Directions: From I-5 take the NE 45th St. exit 169 and head west on NE 45th St. Turn left on Wallingford Ave. N. The bakery is on your right in the first block next to Julia's of Wallingford.

Sultan Bakery

Location: Sultan
Owners: Daryle and Carol Jacobson
Address: 711 Stevens Pass Highway, Sultan
Phone: 793-2434
Hours: Mon-Thurs 6am-5pm; Fri-Sun 6am-7pm
Ride: 17
Directions: From I-5 take I-520 east to I-405 and head north. Take the Monroe exit 23 from I-405 and head east on SR 522 to Monroe. From SR 522 turn left onto SR 2 and head east to Sultan. The bakery is on your left soon after you cross the bridge with a big "Bakery" sign out front.

Sweet Life Cafe

Location: Snohomish
Owners: Paula Inman and Dennis Lebow
Address: 1024 1st St. #201, Snohomish
Phone: 568-3554
Hours: Tues-Sat 9am-9pm; Sun 9am-5pm; **closed Monday**
Rides: 15, 23 and 24
Directions: From I-5 take the SR 2 Snohomish exit 194. Take the first Snohomish exit from SR 2 and follow it into the business district. Take a right on Ave. D and left on 1st St. The bakery is in a three story stone building in the middle of the old town.

Three Girls Bakery

Location:	Pike Place Market, Seattle
Owner:	Jack Levy
Address:	1514 Pike Place, Stall # 1, Seattle
Phone:	622-1045
Hours:	Mon-Sat 7am-6pm; **closed Sunday**
Ride:	7
Directions:	From I-5 take the Stewart St. exit 167. Go straight to Pike Place.

Tio's Bakery and Cafe

Location:	Eastlake Neighborhood, Seattle
Owner:	Carlos Penhuela
Address:	2379 Eastlake Ave. E, Seattle
Phone:	325-0081
Hours:	Mon-Thurs 7am-7pm; Fri-Sat 7am-Midnight; Sun 8am-4pm
Ride:	7

Directions: From I-5 take the NE 45th St. exit 169. Turn right on NE 45th St. and then right again on Roosevelt Ave. NE. Continue south across the University Bridge onto Eastlake Ave. E. Tio's is about one mile south of the bridge on the right.

Upper Crust Bakery

Location:	Magnolia Neighborhood, Seattle
Owner:	Peter Larson
Address:	3204 W McGraw St., Seattle
Phone:	283-1003
Hours:	Mon-Sat 7am-5:30pm; **closed Sunday**
Ride:	3

Directions: From I-5 take the NE 45th St. exit 169 and head west. Turn left on Stone Way N, right on N 34th St., left on Fremont Ave. N across the Fremont Bridge, right on Nickerson St. and keep in the right lane approaching the Ballard Bridge. Go under the Ballard Bridge and head south on 15th Ave. W. Turn right on the Magnolia Bridge. Follow W Galer St. and turn right on 32nd Ave. W. The bakery is on the corner of 32nd Ave. W. and W. McGraw St.

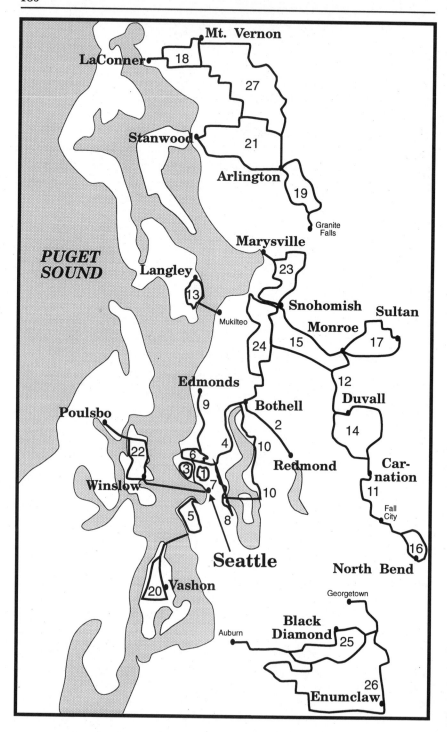

APPENDIX B

CONNECTING RIDES

The rides in this book range from 4 miles to 54 miles. For some readers even the longest ride may be too easy. If this is true for you, there are many ways that you can combine rides to make longer rides as outlined below. You can also lengthen the rides by riding to the start from your home.

Use the map on the opposite page to assist in seeing how the rides connect. The following is the best combination of rides.

RIDE 1
QUEEN ANNE VIEWS TO:

RIDE 3: MAGNIFICENT MAGNOLIA

Adds about 10 miles for a total of 14.6 miles.
From milepost 3.9 of Ride 1, turn right on 9th Ave. W and follow arterial downhill to W Dravus St. Cross 15th Ave. W and turn right on 20th Ave. W, intersecting Ride 3 at milepost 6.5. To return, follow connecting route in reverse.

RIDE 3
MAGNIFICENT MAGNOLIA TO:

RIDE 1: QUEEN ANNE VIEWS

Adds about 7 miles for a total of 15.8 miles.
From milepost 6.5 of Ride 3, turn right on W Dravus St. and cross 15th Ave. W. Climb steep hills of Queen Anne up to milepost 3.9 on Ride 1. To return, follow connecting route in reverse.

RIDE 4
BURKE-GILMAN BREEZE TO:

RIDE 2: DO THE SAMMAMISH SLOUGH

Adds 18.6 miles for a total of 57.2.

A natural extension to the Burke-Gilman Trail is to continue east on the Sammamish Slough Trail. On Ride 4, milepost 18.6, stay on the trail and you will be at milepost 0.2 of Ride 2. Do the Sammamish Slough out-and-back, then reconnect to the Burke-Gilman Trail.

RIDE 24: SWEET SNOHOMISH

Adds 40.3 miles for a total of 78.9.

This is a great ride where you start in the city and travel into the country and back. The Sweet Snohomish extension is much more difficult than riding the Burke-Gilman. On your return trip you will appreciate the flatness of the Burke-Gilman Trail. From the turnaround point of Ride 4 (Burke-Gilman Breeze, milepost 19.8 at the Hillcrest Bakery), follow the route description for Ride 24, Sweet Snohomish. Ride 24 will bring you back to the Hillcrest Bakery where you can reconnect to the Burke-Gilman Trail.

RIDE 5
WEST SEATTLE TOUR TO:

RIDE 20: VASHON VANQUISHED

Adds 26.9 miles for a total of 35.3 miles.

This is a great way to get to Vashon without having to drive to Fauntleroy. From Ride 5, milepost 4.4, turn left on Beach Dr. SW and follow it into Lincoln Park. At the south end of Lincoln Park is a paved path that leads back to Fauntleroy Ave. SW. This is the start of Ride 20, Vashon Vanquished. When you get back from your ride on Vashon Island, retrace your tire tracks to return to Ride 5.

RIDE 6
NORTH SEATTLE LOOP TO:

Ride 1: QUEEN ANNE VIEWS

Adds 6.8 miles for a total of 19.1 miles.

From milepost 8.7 of Ride 6, head south on Fremont Ave. N across the Fremont Bridge. Turn right on Florentia St. and left on 3rd Ave. N. up a long hill. Turn right on W. McGraw St. and go six blocks. The McGraw St. Bakery is on your left. Follow the route description for Ride 1 until milepost 3.2 where you should turn right on 3rd Ave. N back down the hill. At the bottom, turn right on Florentia St. and left on Fremont Ave. N to return to Ride 6.

RIDE 3: MAGNIFICENT MAGNOLIA

Adds 9.8 for a total of 22.1 miles.

From milepost 5.4 on Ride 6, continue south on 24th Ave. NW and turn right on NW Market St. Turn left into the entrance of the Hiram M. Chittenden Locks and **walk** your bicycle across the locks to W Commodore Way. You are now at milepost 8.3 on Ride 3. Return the way you came to get back on Ride 6.

RIDE 7: DOWNTOWN DELIGHTS

Adds 15.7 miles for a total of 28 miles.

From milepost 5.4 on Ride 6, continue south on 24th Ave. NW and turn right on NW Market St. Turn left into the entrance of the Hiram M. Chittenden Locks. This is the start of Ride 7. Follow the route description for Ride 7 and then return via the same route back to milepost 5.4 on Ride 6.

RIDE 7
DOWNTOWN DELIGHTS TO:

RIDE 22: ACROSS SOUND VOYAGE

Adds 5.7 to 14.7 miles for a total of 38 to 47 miles.

A great way to begin Ride 22 is to ride downtown to the ferry dock. In the summer time, when the city is full of tourists, it is probably faster to ride downtown than to drive and find a parking place. From the Pike Place Market, go left on Western Ave., right on Yesler, and left on Alaskan Way.

RIDE 11
CARNATION COUNTRY CAPER TO:

RIDE 14: THE CARNA-VALL RIDE

Adds 24.7 miles for a total of 41.5 miles.

Ride 11 will take you to Carnation. To get in some more miles, begin Ride 14 at the Original Brown Bag Restaurant and head north on the Carna-vall loop. You can also continue north from Duvall on Ride 12.

RIDES 11, 14, 12 and 17: FALL CITY to SULTAN and RETURN

For a long tour, start at Fall City and take Ride 11 to Carnation, Ride 14 to Duvall, Ride 12 to Monroe, and Ride 17 to Sultan and return for a total of **85.7 miles**.

RIDES 11, 14, 15 and 23: FALL CITY to MARYSVILLE and RETURN

For a very long tour, start at Fall City and take Ride 11 to Carnation, Ride 14 to Duvall, Ride 15 to Snohomish and Ride 23 to Marysville. This is about a **100 mile** ride.

RIDE 12
MEANDERING TO MONROE TO:

RIDE 15: HIGH BRIDGE ROAD

Adds 19.1 miles for a total of 40.6 miles.

This connection extends an easy ride into a much longer moderate ride. From Ride 12, milepost 5.7, do not cross the Snoqualmie River but continue straight (north) onto High Bridge Road. Follow the route description in Ride 15 starting at milepost 4.6. When you get to Monroe, start at the beginning of the route description for Ride 15 and turn left at milepost 4.6 onto West Snoqualmie River Rd. Follow route description for Ride 12 starting at milepost 15.9.

RIDE 17: SIDE ROADS TO SULTAN

Adds 22.7 miles for a total of 44.2 miles.

Ride 12 takes you to the Sky River Bakery in Monroe. This is the starting location for Ride 17, Side Roads to Sultan. The combination of these two rides makes a great 44 mile jaunt.

RIDE 14
THE CARNA-VALL RIDE TO:

RIDE 12: MEANDERING TO MONROE

Adds 21.5 miles for a total of 46.2 miles.

For a variation on Ride 14, start in Carnation, milepost 13.2, follow the route description for the return to Duvall, and then do Ride 12 to Monroe. The combined rides total 46.2 miles.

RIDE 15
HIGH BRIDGE ROAD TO:

RIDE 23: DOUBLE DUTCH TREAT

Adds 37.1 miles for a total of 61.5 miles.

If you are feeling strong, this is a great long ride from Monroe to Marysville and return. Take Ride 15 to Snohomish and begin Ride 23 to Marysville and back to Snohomish. Then complete Ride 15 for a total of 61.5 miles.

RIDE 16
SNOQUALMIE RIVER TOUR TO:

RIDE 11: CARNATION COUNTRY CAPER

Adds 16.8 miles for a total of 39.1 miles.

Both of these rides start in Fall City. You can link them by simply doing one and then the other. I would suggest doing Ride 16 first as it has more hills and will have less traffic earlier in the day. You can also start Ride 11 in Carnation and link it to Ride 16 in Fall City.

RIDE 19
STILLY FOOTHILLS RAMBLE TO:

RIDE 21: DON'T BE LEFSE BEHIND

Adds 33.7 miles for a total of 61.3 miles.

Ride 19 takes you from Granite Falls to Arlington. From Arlington take Ride 21 to Stanwood and return to Arlington. Then follow Ride 19 description back to Granite Falls.

RIDE 27: OVER THE HILL

Adds 52.9 miles for a total of 80.5 miles.

The combination of Rides 19 and 27 produces a long, challenging ride, from Granite Falls to Mt. Vernon and back. Take Ride 19 from Granite Falls to

Arlington. Stop at the Country Bakery and then take Ride 27 Over the Hill to Mt. Vernon and return. You may want to stop at the Country Bakery again before you head back to Granite Falls.

RIDE 24
SWEET SNOHOMISH TO:

RIDE 15: HIGH BRIDGE ROAD

Adds 21 miles for a total of 61.3.
The ride from Bothell to Snohomish, Ride 24, is a good hard ride. To make it even longer, from Snohomish start Ride 15 from "THE RETURN" location, milepost 16. Then start at the beginning of the Ride 15 route description and go to milepost 12.4. Instead of turning right on Broadway, turn left on Broadway and pick up the route description for Ride 24 beginning at milepost 26.2.

RIDE 23: DOUBLE DUTCH TREAT

Adds 37.1 miles for a total of 77.4 miles.
Ride 24 takes you from Bothell to Snohomish. You can add an additional 37.1 miles by starting Ride 23 once you get to Snohomish and riding to Marysville and back.

RIDE 27
OVER THE HILL TO:

RIDE 18: TULIP TOWN TOUR

Adds 28.7 miles for a total of 81.6 miles.
Start in Arlington and ride over the hill to Mt. Vernon. From Mt. Vernon, relax with a flat ride out to LaConner on Ride 18. On the return of Ride 18, at milepost 22.5, continue straight and follow the route description for Ride 27 from milepost 31.1.

Fred Wert enjoying bicycling.

ABOUT THE AUTHOR

For more than 20 years, Fred Wert has bicycled extensively around Puget Sound. Some of his first miles were logged as a Category II racer during the 1970's. During the 1980's and into the 90's, his pace slowed a bit but he still managed to pedal almost every road in the state. In 1982, ever intrigued by the new and the novel, Fred added mountain bicycling to his activities. His greatest accomplishment in that area came when he rode the rugged Washington Cross-State trail in less than five days.

Lest you think Fred is always out playing, much of his time is devoted to bicycle advocacy. Since 1975 he has been a member of Cascade Bicycle Club and served on the Government Affairs Committee for many years. He is currently a board member of the Backcountry Bicycle Trails Club and heads their efforts in developing new mountain bicycle trails. To top it all off, Fred works on promoting and developing new rail-trails throughout the northwest to ensure that abandoned railroad corridors will be preserved for bicycling and other recreational uses. He is author of *Washington's Rail-Trails: A Guide for Walkers, Bicyclists and Equestrians,* published by the Mountaineers, which provides details on 40 rail-trails throughout the state.

Believe it or not, Fred does think about some things besides bicycling (and occasionally bakeries). He also loves kayaking, mountaineering, skiing and piloting small planes. All of these activities are much improved, he claims, when undertaken in the company of good friends (a fact he took advantage of in researching this book).

On a more serious or perhaps professional note, Fred is a board member of the Washington Wildlife and Recreation Coalition, which promotes the public ownership of land for recreation and preservation. He also has his own consulting business, which requires that he occasionally spend very large amounts of time with his computer. Fortunately, Fred is married to a tolerant and athletic woman with a great sense of humor. They make their home in the Green Lake area of Seattle.

BAKERIES BY BICYCLE

A Guide to
Puget Sound's Best Bakeries

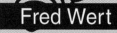

Fred Wert

BAKERIES BY BICYCLE

ORDER FORM

Who needs a copy of this book?
Everyone who loves to eat great pastries!
Anyone who loves to ride a bicycle!
Order additional copies for your family and friends, today.

Name: _____

Address: _____

City:_____ State:_____ Zip:_____

BAKERIES BY BICYCLE

Quantity: _____ @ $10.95 each   _____
Sales Tax (Washington residents only):
    add $.90 per copy   _____
Shipping and handling:
    $1.50 first book, $1.00/additional   _____

    TOTAL enclosed   _____

Make checks payable to Infinity Press
and mail to:
Infinity Press
P.O. 31204
Seattle, WA 98103-1204